Praise for

THE INFLUENCING MACHINE

W9-BRB-018

"Hilarious and levelheaded." — *The New Yorker*

"One of the coolest and most charming book releases of this year. . . . [T]hink *The Information* meets *The Medium is the Massage* meets *Everything Explained Through Flowcharts*. . . . *The Influencing Machine* takes a refreshingly alternative approach to the age-old issue of why we disparage and distrust the news."
— Kirstin Butler, *The Atlantic*

"This is one of those books that feels like the author has been working up to it for her whole life, distilling all her varied experience and insight into one mind-opening, thought-provoking, and incredibly timely volume. . . . An absolutely spectacular read."
— Cory Doctorow, *BoingBoing*

"Exhaustively researched, elegantly argued, and stylishly illustrated by Neufeld in a way that gives a guiding simplicity to even its headiest ideas, *The Influencing Machine* is a singular piece of contemporary media criticism." — John Semley, *The A.V. Club*

"NPR's Gladstone is so remarkable as a commentator, and Neufeld so brilliant as a graphic artist, that all you can do is laugh and be amazed at the clarity of her commentary." — Lena Tabori, *Huffpost Books*

"Enthralling." — Ray Olson, *Booklist*

"*The Influencing Machine* is more than graphic nonfiction. It's a media studies course in itself." — *Cartoon Movement*

"Like Malcolm Gladwell or Michael Lewis or Michael Pollan, Brooke somehow takes a subject most of us don't give a damn about and makes it completely entertaining."
— Ira Glass, host of *This American Life*

"Gladstone . . . and noted illustrator Neufeld . . . make a formidable pair in this fascinating history of media's influence. . . . An indispensible guide to our ever-evolving media landscape that's brought vividly to life." — *Publishers Weekly*, starred review

"Gladstone has nailed it by opting for a comic-book format for her first book, *The Influencing Machine*; the images work as a puckish counterpoint to occasionally abstract discussions, as well as sobering reminders of the real-world consequences of the media's misdeeds." — Laura Miller, *Salon*

"Though the graphic format employed here is often playful and always reader friendly, this analysis of contemporary journalism is as incisive as it is entertaining, while offering a lesson on good citizenship through savvy media consumption."

—*Kirkus Reviews*, starred review

"Neufeld uses expressionistic panels to tease complexity out of Gladstone's sharp point."

—Dan Kois, *New York Times*

"*The Influencing Machine* is an indispensable guidebook for anyone who hopes to navigate the mirages and constantly shifting sands of our media landscape. Brooke Gladstone's text and Josh Neufeld's images illuminate one another with crackling wit and intelligence."

—Alison Bechdel, author of *Fun Home*
and *The Essential Dykes to Watch Out For*

"Brooke Gladstone's *The Influencing Machine* is so remarkable that it is hard to describe. The best I can do is: it's a book about the history and current controversies of the media, all done as a Spiegelman-style comic-strip narrative. Brooke herself (or at least an avatar) leads you through it all, and her 'voice'—well known after her years as host of NPR's *On the Media*—comes through loud and clear, thanks to Josh Neufeld's witty drawings. I learned a lot, including a lot that I should have known already, and enjoyed every minute."

—Michael Kinsley

"A first-rate comics manifesto. *The Influencing Machine* has influenced me to think much more deeply about the media landscape we live in. Gladstone and Neufeld can show and tell with the best of 'em."

—Scott McCloud, author of *Understanding Comics*

"Think Art Spiegelman meets Marshall McLuhan."

—Leon Neyfakh, *New York Observer*

"*The Influencing Machine* seems birthed from the same graphic novel universe as Daniel Clowes, Harvey Pekar and the Hernandez brothers with their skeptical, soulful slackers and alt-take on the world."

—Felicia Feaster, *Arts Critic ATL*

"A visual tour de force."

—John Pavlus

"An incisive and engaging look at the mainstream media, its evolution and its biases."

—*Time Out New York*

"Often brilliant and always thought-provoking."

—*Graphic Novel Reporter*

"A great book."

—Stephen Colbert

THE
INFLUENCING
MACHINE

THE
INFLUENCING

MACHINE

BROOKE GLADSTONE ON THE MEDIA

ILLUSTRATED BY JOSH NEUFELD

WITH ADDITIONAL PENCILING BY RANDY JONES AND SUSANN FERRIS-JONES

W. W. NORTON & COMPANY

NEW YORK   LONDON

Most of the words spoken herein by actual people are drawn from historical documents, transcripts, or interviews. Ellipses are used to indicate both pauses and internal edits... Great care was taken to ensure that no remark was taken out of context.

For information about permission to reproduce selections from this book, write to Permissions, W. W. Norton & Company, Inc., 500 Fifth Avenue, New York, NY 10110

For information about special discounts for bulk purchases, please contact W. W. Norton Special Sales at specialsales@wwnorton.com or 800-233-4830

Manufacturing by Courier Westford
Book design by Neil Swaab
Production manager: Anna Oler

Library of Congress Cataloging-in-Publication Data

Gladstone, Brooke.
The influencing machine : Brooke Gladstone on the media / illustrated by Josh Neufeld ; with additional penciling by Randy Jones and Susann Ferris-Jones. — 1st ed.
    p. cm.
   Includes bibliographical references.
   ISBN 978-0-393-07779-7 (hardcover)
1. Journalism—Comic books, strips, etc. 2. Broadcast journalism—Comic books, strips, etc. 3. Gladstone, Brooke—Comic books, strips, etc. 4. Graphic novels. I. Neufeld, Josh. II. Jones, Randy, 1950– III. Jones, Susann. IV. Title.
   PN4731.G53 2011
   302.23—dc22   2011009820

ISBN: 978-0-393-34246-8 pbk.

W. W. Norton & Company, Inc.
500 Fifth Avenue, New York, N.Y. 10110
www.wwnorton.com

W. W. Norton & Company Ltd.
Castle House, 75/76 Wells Street, London W1T 3QT

4 5 6 7 8 9 0

To Fred, Sophie, and Maxine
—B. G.

To Sari and Phoebe
—J. N.

CONTENTS

INTRODUCTION

MEET *the* **AUTHOR**

I am Brooke Gladstone, and I am a reporter.

Hello, Brooke.

I like to pry.

I like people to tell me important stuff. Complicated stuff. Personal stuff, sometimes.

I even kinda like it when they cry. I can't help it. I'm a radio reporter.

And then, if they let me, I tell everyone else.

I have compulsions...

Tell us about them, Brooke...

First let me tell you about a dream this friend of mine had when he was in college.

Okay.

He's dreaming that he hears a riot in the street. Some kind of demonstration.

So he goes to the window, and leans out, and watches. That's all. He just watches.

He likes to watch?

That's when he realized he was a reporter. Now he has a Pulitzer Prize.

Anna Quindlen* has a Pulitzer, too. She once said that "being a reporter is as much a diagnosis as a job description." Not true for everyone, but...

...Compulsions?

*Author, former New York Times columnist and contributor to Newsweek.

Well, I can't really process things unless I'm reporting them, know what I mean?

Not really...

Like when the Twin Towers fell -- my station was nearby. We had to evacuate.

And my show was suspended for a week...

...so I couldn't report it. Couldn't explain it to other people. So I couldn't explain it to myself. My head almost exploded.

But when my mother died...

I recorded it.

And that was a relief.

So maybe that's what I get out of **making** media. But what do we get out of **consuming** media? Especially news media?

WE HUNGER FOR OBJECTIVITY, but increasingly swallow "news" like Jell-O shots in ad hoc cyber-saloons. We marinate in punditry seasoned with only those facts and opinions we can digest without cognitive distress.

Sometimes we feel a little queasy about it— queasiness we project back onto the media.

But we don't really get agitated until we encounter the *other guys'* media. Those guys are consuming lies. They are getting juiced up. Their media diet is making them stupid.

What if *our* media choices are making *us* stupid? What if they're shortening *our* attention span, exciting our lusts, eroding our values, hobbling our judgment?

I've been reporting on the media for some 25 years, apparently *none* of them *good* years. The concentration of media ownership, the blurring of news and opinion, the yawning news hole (there's teeth in there!) created by 24-hour news cycles . . . scarifying local coverage . . . shriveled foreign coverage . . . liberal bias . . . conservative bias . . . celebrities . . . scandal . . . echo chambers . . . arrogance . . . elitism . . . bloggers with *no standards* . . .

I see our most hallowed journalistic institutions crumbling, I see the business model that relied on mass audiences being displaced, with stunning speed, by one that survives by aggregating millions of tiny, targeted audience fragments.

The reality that anyone with a cell phone can now presume to make, break, or *fabricate* the news has shaken our citadels of culture and journalism to the core. The once mighty gatekeepers watch in horror as libelous, manifestly unprofessional websites flood the media ether with unadulterated id.

Terrifying. I can't wait to watch it play out.

See, I **don't** believe that the convulsions roiling the media augur the apocalypse.

WE'VE BEEN HERE BEFORE:

the incivility, the inanities, the obsessions, and the broken business models. In fact, it's been far *worse* and the Republic survives.

The irony is that the more people participate in the media, the more they hate the media. The greater the participation, the greater the paranoia that the media are in control.

But I've watched journalists cover countless catastrophes, elections, political gridlock, moral panics, and several wars. I've seen how public opinion coalesces around the issues dominating the news, and I can tell you that *no one* is in control.

There is no conspiracy. Even though the media are mostly corporate-owned, their first allegiance is to their public because, if they lose that allegiance, they lose *money*.

Sometimes the press leads the public; sometimes the public leads the press. The media, at least the mainstream media, don't *want* to get too far ahead. They just don't want to be left behind.

Conspiratorial? That's a joke. *Craven?* Not quite so funny.

Once I was confronted by a gaggle of high-ranking Chinese journalists who pointed to several instances in which American news outlets pulled their punches when reporting on the Bush administration and the Iraq war. They said that proved the American media were afraid of the government.

That's ridiculous, I replied. The American media are not afraid of the government. They are afraid of their audiences and advertisers. The media do not control you. They pander to you.

That's how I landed on my central metaphor...

...and the title of this book.

THE INFLUENCING MACHINE "Patient Zero"

Since the industrial age began, there has been the recurring delusion that an evil machine is controlling our minds.

The first known case occurred in England three years after French royals Louis XVI and Marie Antoinette lost their heads.

On December 30, 1796, in the House of Commons, debate is leading to a declaration of war with France. Tea merchant James Tilly Matthews is determined to stop it.

...so I say France has no desire for peace!

Can't breathe... can't... think ... the Air Loom... infects me .... such pain... agghh... must speak... James... SPEAK... NOW!

TREASON!

?

Shortly...

Another poor nutter for Bedlam.

So it seems you are mad.

You cannot understand.

Try me.

As you wish...

The minds of powerful men are being controlled by a diabolical machine, fueled by **cesspool stench, dog effluvia, human seminal fluid,** and **horse flatulence...**

I call it the Air Loom.

It weaves and magnetizes the gases, which are then released to plague its victim with grotesque visions, poison his dreams, confound his reason, and drive him to war.

See how the Air Loom uses the new "science of gases?" Influencing Machines always incorporate the latest scientific breakthroughs of their eras.

It uses **"fluid-locking"** to freeze the tongues of politicians...

"Kiteing" to fix an alien idea in the mind where it "undulates" for hours, pushing all other ideas aside...

...and **"lobster-cracking"** to kill its victims.

Usually, Matthews is cogent and reasonable, but he never wavers in his belief in the Air Loom. He is Patient Zero, the first of many to be tormented by an Influencing Machine. But the syndrome has yet to be given its name.

"Whenever he strikes the machine, my body breaks."

"Whenever he twists the dial, my head aches..."

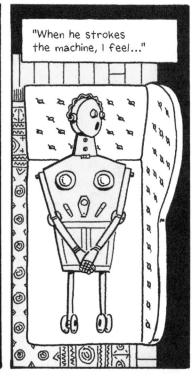

"When he strokes the machine, I feel..."

"My mother is controlled by a machine, too. So are my friends. But they don't know it, they can't see it. I can't bear it. I want to run away."

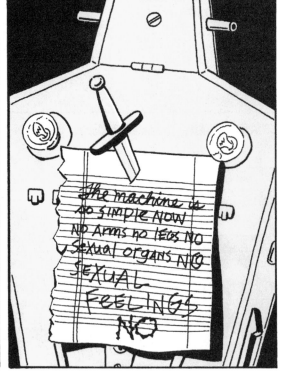

The machine is so simple now no arms no legs no sexual organs no sexual feelings no

THE MEDIA MACHINE IS A DELUSION.

What we're really dealing with is a *mirror*: an exalting, degrading, tedious, and transcendent funhouse mirror of America.

Actually, media is a plural noun: we're dealing with a whole mess of mirrors.

They aren't well calibrated; they're fogged, and cracked. But you're in there, reflected somewhere, and so is everyone else (including people you dislike).

The media landscape is so cluttered with mirrors facing mirrors that we can't tell where an image begins or ends.

By the way, in the coming years that clutter is going to get a lot worse. In the near future, we'll carry our information technology, not just in our hands, but *inside* us—in the form of implants.

I'm not crazy—just ask the propeller-heads over at the MIT Media Lab or the geeks polled by the Pew Internet & American Life Project.

Right now we are tumbling through a technological wormhole and when we come out the other side, our thoughts will spill seamlessly into cyberspace with the potential to influence minds everywhere.

So when we see ourselves distorted in the media mirror, we should probably consider that some of what we see is actually us.

We're seduced by celebrity stories. We enjoy a good car chase.

And who doesn't take guilty pleasure in the refreshing saliva spray of a commentator spouting our views?

Back in 1922, Walter Lippmann wrote...

"Let him cast a stone who **never** passed on as the real inside truth what he had heard someone say who knew no more than he did."

"For the **real** environment is altogether too big, too complex, and too fleeting for direct acquaintance."

"And although we have to act in that environment, we have to **reconstruct** it on a simpler model before we can manage with it."

But now, with most of the media's resources at our fingertips, we can seek **beyond** mediated interpretations of events.

We can choose how **much** to simplify our worldview.

When coverage is contradictory or confusing, we can read the original documents, or track down a dubious claim to its **source**...

...or seek sensible views **outside** our comfort zone.

It's risky. As John Dewey once said, "Anyone who has begun to think places some portion of the world in **jeopardy**."

But, as Spider-Man once said (quoting his Uncle Ben): "With great power comes great **responsibility**."

THE
INFLUENCING
MACHINE

"In the Beginning..."

...there are no journalists. But in every place written language emerges -- Sumaria, Egypt, China -- you can find... **publicists.**

Consider ancient Guatemala.

First the Mayan royalty develop writing...

...then they hire publicists (**scribes**) to generate some primordial P.R.

As the eons pass and literacy spreads, a few extraordinary people use the written word to relate history.

HISTORIES by HERODOTUS OF HALIKARNASSUS

And a few of the brighter ancient rulers realize that **actual news** -- handled right -- could work better than pure P.R.

EUREKA!

Case in point: Julius Caesar decrees that the activities of the Roman Senate be posted on a handwritten sheet... called the Acta Diurna ("Daily Acts").

ACTA DIVRNA

That's because the Senate debates and votes behind closed doors, and he figures a little exposure could rob it of the mystique that **secrecy** confers.

Plus -- when the Acta Diurna is copied and sent to Rome's provincial governors, they stay connected to the capital.

News serves as **glue**, sticking the far-flung empire together.

Inevitably, the focus of the Acta Diurna drifts from the political to the personal: divorce, crime. **Orgies.**

"Verba volant scripta manent."*

Ah, the Golden Age!

ACTA DIVRNA
CALIGVLA CVTS VP

*"Words fly away, writings remain."-- Cato Titus at the Roman Senate

As information technology advances (kudos, Gutenberg) and control begins to pass from the powerful to the plebs, the powerful grow decidedly less enthusiastic about it.

By the 17th century, many urban Europeans can rely on weekly or even some daily papers for news of the world.

But not the news of the country in which they're printed.

That's because printers operate at the pleasure of the authorities, and the authorities do not find local coverage pleasurable.

First, England bans newspapers for six years. Parliament rules that every printed word must be approved -- licensed -- **before** publication. In 1644, **John Milton** complains.

We must not think to make a **commodity** of all the knowledge in the Land, to mark and license it like our broad cloth, and our wool packs.

Believe it, Lords and Commons, they who counsel ye to such a suppressing, do as good as bid ye suppress yourselves.

AREOPAGITICA,
A
SPEECH
OF
Mr. JOHN MILTON
For the Liberty of UNLICENC'D
PRINTING.
To the PARLIAMENT of ENGLAND

LONDON 1644

He is ignored for 51 years.

Eventually the courts revoke prior restraint, but printers can still be ruined by the charge of "seditious libel" for publishing criticism of the government.

And truth is no defense. Legal doctrine holds that "the greater the truth the greater the libel" --

...the greater the threat to Divine Right.

Rulers see ink-stained barbarians at the gate... and hunker down.

The American Exception

1 In New York, printer John Peter Zenger is charged with seditious *libel* for publishing criticism of the King's governor.

His lawyer, the eminent Andrew (not Alexander) Hamilton, unexpectedly seeks to offer truth as a defense...

...for would it not be a sad case if the judges, for want of due information, should give as severe a judgment against a man for publishing truth, as for publishing lies?

Mr. Hamilton, you know the truth of a libel cannot be admitted into evidence.

Hamilton appeals to the jury to ignore the judges and nullify the law.

It is not the cause of one poor printer alone you are now trying. No! It affects every free man that lives under a British government in America.

It is the best cause. It is the cause of liberty.

NOT GUILTY.

Henceforth, truth may be used as a defense against libel... in the American colonies.

It takes England another 108 years.

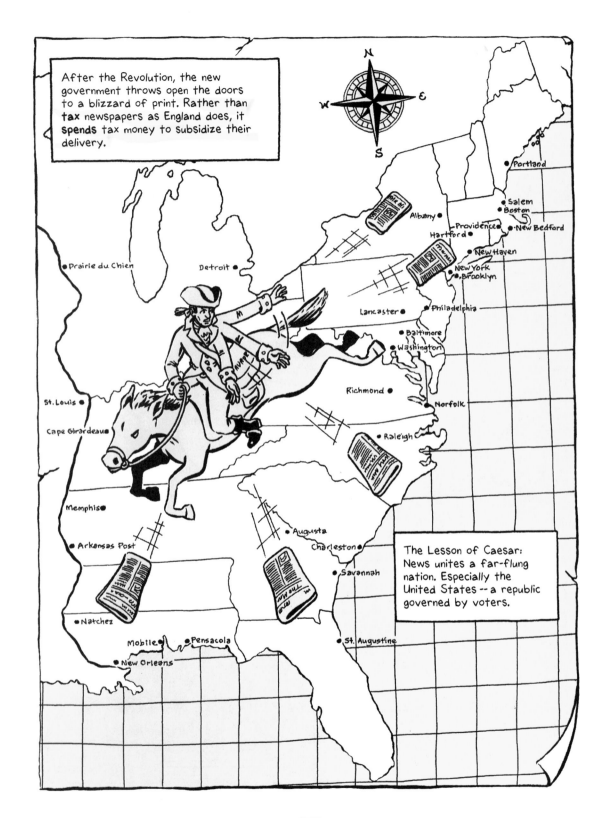

After the Revolution, the new government throws open the doors to a blizzard of print. Rather than **tax** newspapers as England does, it **spends** tax money to subsidize their delivery.

The Lesson of Caesar: News unites a far-flung nation. Especially the United States -- a republic governed by voters.

In 1798, America is embroiled in an "undeclared Naval War with France" -- our **first** undeclared war!

Paranoia sweeps Washington.

President John Adams signs the **Alien and Sedition Acts.**

The Alien part says he can deport any foreigner deemed "dangerous."

It's never enforced. (The French mostly scram.)

13

Newspapers savaged Adams during his first term. So when he runs again, he uses the Sedition Act to jail editors who favor his rival, Vice President Thomas Jefferson.

A critic in Jefferson's pay writes that Adams has a "hideous hermaphroditic character." Meanwhile, pro-Adams papers slime Jefferson as an incest-loving libertine.

It's the original negative campaign.

The Connecticut COURANT.

TOM ROBS WIDOWS!

THE TRUE AMERICAN

TOOTHLESS ADAMS

NORFOLK GAZETTE

JEFFERSON GODLESS JACOBIN

T.J. A HALFBREED

T.J. A HALFBREED

Aurora

ADAMS THE MOCK MONARCH

Aurora

ADAMS THE MOCK MONARCH

The Sedition Act expires when Jefferson becomes President.

FREE PRESS

He writes this in 1799.

Our citizens may be deceived for a while, and have been deceived; but as long as the **presses** can be protected, we may trust to them for light.

He writes this in 1807.

Nothing can now be believed which is seen in a newspaper. Truth itself becomes suspicious by being put into that **polluted vehicle**.

What happened to Tom?

In 1801, Tom becomes President.

The press hates presidents.

Hmmm..."It is well known that the man, whom it delighteth the people to honor, keeps, and for many years has kept, as his concubine, one of his slaves. Her name is **Sally**. The name of her eldest son is **Tom**. His features are said to bear a striking resemblance to the President himself..."

From the start, American newspapers boil over with brilliant analysis and passionate advocacy.

They also churn with vicious, personal accusations, some of which are true.

But the truth is irrelevant. Lying journalists helped build this country.

Flashback --1768: Samuel Adams, brewer's son and Boston Gazette editor, is **that** kind of journalist. Desperately seeking revolution...

He concocts stories about British soldiers violating patriot women...

He plans the Boston Tea Party...

He celebrates violence against British loyalists.

Journalistically speaking, he is **not ethical**.

Neither is Jefferson. While serving as George Washington's dissenting Secretary of State, he's peeved when Treasury Secretary Alexander Hamilton uses Treasury funds to start a paper supporting Washington's policies. (Not as un-kosher then as it is today.)

So Jefferson **steals** State Department money to fund a paper opposing them. (Totally un-kosher.)

And he leaves his office door unlocked, so his editor can slip in, read the reports left on his desk, and then quote them out of context to make the White House look bad.

Did Jefferson invent the **political leak**, a practice so abhorred it has sparked criminal trials, and even prison terms?!

Of course not.

George Washington did.

Washington deployed Cabinet and military officials to wine, dine, and feed information to certain reporters if they agreed to report the President's way.

What's the problem? He never told a lie.

All his life, Jefferson deplores the **"putrid state"** of newspapers while **defending** their right to be putrid.

Even after 50 years of often-feculent press freedom, he never wavers in his belief that the sole defense against tyranny is unfettered speech.

The only security of all is in a free press. The force of public opinion cannot be resisted when permitted freely to be expressed. The **agitation** it produces must be submitted to. It is necessary, to keep the waters **pure**.

Across the water, politicians are terrified of agitation, convinced that tremors will crumble the very foundations of government. But rigidity has a cost...

...It limits how high a structure can reach.

SKYSCRAPERS ARE BUILT WITH RIGID CENTRAL CORES, but also the *flexibility* to sway in high winds. Likewise, Jeffersonian democracy (he *was* an architect) is designed to withstand tempests as it ascends, building freedom upon freedom.

Its *resilience* is guaranteed by representative government.

Its *strength* derives from the First Amendment, which enables voters to know each other, assess their leaders and gauge the state of the nation.

SPEECH ITSELF, inevitable and unrelenting, is the wind. It can dance like a zephyr.

It can roar or shriek or wail. But it can't be stopped.

Everything we hate about the media today was present at its creation: its corrupt or craven practitioners, its easy manipulation by the powerful, its capacity for propagating lies, its penchant for amplifying rage.

Also present was everything we admire—and require—from the media: factual information, penetrating analysis, probing investigation, truth spoken to power.

Same as it ever was.

AMERICAN GOVERNMENTS WILL ALWAYS LASH OUT at discordant speech when they feel

threatened, either by an external enemy or by an enemy within—and no one who can write or speak is immune from its sting.

The press is merely the loudest canary in the coal mine.

Of course, governments reasonably argue that when the nation faces a mortal threat, certain rights must be suspended, and in such times many citizens agree.

But civil libertarians argue back that the nation is equally threatened by the suspension of rights that *define* us.

Their argument is not just about what we learn of the conduct of government when speech is free, but what we learn of ourselves.

Even more, it's about what we *think* of ourselves when speech is free.

The Constitution makes no distinction between the speech of a fractious, self-interested, fitfully heroic *people* and its fractious, self-interested, fitfully heroic *press*. That's because there never really was a distinction, and now that everyone carries a potential printing press in a back pocket or purse, there's no use pretending that there is.

So what follows is a brief history of speech suppression in America.

It has a happy ending. Two steps forward usually follow each step backward. We learn from our mistakes. Then we forget and learn again.

Existential Angst

I quit, boys!

Must I shoot a simple-minded soldier who deserts, while I must not touch a hair of a wily agitator who induces him to desert?

HURL KING LINCOLN FROM HIS THRONE

BROTHERS LAY DOWN YOUR ARMS

The Lincoln White House shutters, for a spell, some 300 opposition newspapers. It censors war dispatches sent by telegraph.

As America enters the First World War, Woodrow Wilson signs the 1917 Espionage Act, outlawing virtually any speech that could be deemed to "harm the war effort."

ADAMS

Then he signs the Sedition Act -- 1798 all over again. It's illegal to print, write, or even **speak** disloyal words about the President, the Congress, the flag, the military, its uniforms, war bonds...

Fun Fact: In United States v. Motion Picture Film "The Spirit of '76" (1917), a federal court censors a film about the Revolutionary War because it depicts Redcoats committing atrocities, thereby undermining support for our British ally.

The producer is sentenced to ten years in prison.

In 1938, Congress convenes the first session of the House Un-American Activities Committee.

Chairman Martin Dies is supposed to track Nazi propaganda...

≷ Yawn ≷

...but mostly he chases Communists. Under suspicion: 483 newspapers, 280 labor groups, the Boy Scouts...

...and Shirley Temple.

Never participate in **anything** ... without consulting the American Legion or your local Chamber of Commerce.

In 1940, Franklin D. Roosevelt signs the Smith Act, making it a criminal offense to advocate "overthrowing the government."

Later, the Act is used to convict Socialists and Communists. Marx and Lenin said that communism can't prevail unless capitalism is **violently** overthrown. Therefore, say the prosecutors, **all** Communists will "speedily" attempt revolution.

No need to prove the defendants actually plan to revolt. It is **ideas** -- not actions -- that pose the existential threat.

After the war, Senator Joe McCarthy rides to fame on the Red Scare, spurring loyalty oaths, blacklists, book-burnings...

I have in my hand a list of 205 cases of individuals who appear to be either card-carrying members or certainly loyal to the Communist Party...

He investigates the State Department, the U.N., Voice of America, the CIA, universities, artists, journalists. Some people lose their jobs. Some finger their friends. A few kill themselves.

Then in April 1954, he investigates the Army, alienating President Eisenhower, a retired five-star general. McCarthy isn't worried. He had wrestled with Harry Truman too, and it didn't slow him down.

Tuning in to the fledgling ABC network, 20 million spellbound Americans watch for **36 days** -- as the Senator slings mud and scorn at witnesses.

Army lawyer Joseph Welch testifies on Day 30.

Have you no sense of decency, sir? At long last, have you left no **sense of decency**?

I know this hurts you, Mr. Welch.

Senator, I think it hurts you, too, sir.

McCarthy's popularity plunges. A few months later, the Senate condemns him.

Historians argue over how much to credit television for McCarthy's downfall.

We must not confuse **dissent** with **disloyalty**...

McCarthy had crusaded, unchecked, for nearly five years. Then, just before the hearings, CBS newsman Edward R. Murrow signaled a shift in the wind.

We will not be driven by **fear**.... If we dig deep in our history and our doctrine, and remember that we are not descended from fearful men...

For six weeks on ABC, that wind takes on gale force and suddenly -- poof! -- Senator McCarthy just seems to... blow away.

But how long might it have taken...

McCarthyism is **Americanism** with its sleeves rolled.

...had the nation not had the chance to look deep into his eyes and see a savage reflection of itself staring back?

For Lyndon Johnson, no controversial sedition bills, no noisy debates, no overt muzzling of critics. He lives in the television age.

Instead, he quietly backs new FBI programs to infiltrate and disrupt the activities of dissenters, and illegally expands the CIA's role to spy on radicals and peace activists.

Johnson fights a two-front war and loses both, crushed by the inexhaustible stream of North Vietnamese guerrillas and grisly TV footage from the battlefield. Then in '68: his own Dien Bien Phu...

To say that we are mired in **stalemate** seems the only realistic ... conclusion. The only rational way out ... will be to **negotiate**, not as victors, but as an honorable people...

If I've lost Cronkite, I've lost Middle America.

A few weeks later, Johnson announces he won't seek re-election.

When Richard Nixon takes office, he uses Johnson's intelligence apparatus but makes it **personal**, amassing his "enemies list," using IRS audits as weapons, burgling offices.

When the President does it, that means that it is not illegal.

In 1969, military analyst and Pentagon insider Daniel Ellsberg removes 47 volumes from his safe at the RAND Corporation, and with the help of his friend Anthony Russo, copies them.

They are the "Pentagon Papers," a Defense Department study of U.S. involvement in Vietnam: 23 years of secret interventions and lies. Ellsberg, a former Marine, resolves to risk life in prison to end a "wrongful" war.

No one is ever going to tell me again that I have a duty to lie...

After failing to persuade any Senators to expose the Papers, he takes them to the New York Times, which after consideration, begins to publish them.

Monday, June 14th, 1971, 3:09 p.m., the Oval Office. The President and Chief of Staff H. R. Haldeman.

To the ordinary guy, all this is a bunch of gobbledygook. But out of the gobbledygook comes a very clear thing: **You can't trust the government.**

And the implicit infallibility of presidents, which has been an accepted thing in America, is badly hurt by this, because it shows that people do things the President wants to do even though it's wrong, and **the President can be wrong.**

June 17th, 1971, 2:42 p.m., Oval Office. The President, Haldeman, and Press Secretary Ronald Ziegler.

We can **kill** these people with this. "Knowingly publishing stolen goods." That's what the Times is doing... "Giving aid and comfort to the enemy." **That's** the way you have to play it.

Nixon charges Ellsberg and Anthony Russo with treason under the Espionage Act of 1917, and serves the Times with a federal injunction to stop publication.

The charges against Ellsberg and Russo were dropped.

How wouldja like to be the head of the **FBI**?

Someone **broke** into Ellsberg's psychiatrist's office!

Gross governmental misconduct! MISTRIAL!

The New York Times's trial goes all the way to the Supreme Court.

The New York Times

SUPREME COURT, 6-3, UPHOLDS NEWSPAPERS ON PUBLICATION OF THE PENTAGON REPORT
TIMES RESUMES ITS SERIES HALTED 15 DAYS

In revealing the workings of government that led to the Vietnam War, the newspapers nobly did precisely that which the Founders hoped and trusted they would do.

JUSTICE HUGO BLACK

So now, because of the media, we have access to the true history of that war and the chance to **learn** from it. (Not that we necessarily will.)

Meanwhile, a couple of hungry young reporters, Carl Bernstein and Bob Woodward, follow a daisy chain of malfeasance from a break-in... to slush funds... to dirty tricks... to spying... to lying... all the way into the Oval Office.

The Washington Post

Nixon Denies Role in Cover-up, Admits Abuse by Subordinates

Says Tapes' Release Would Be 'Crippling'

So now, because of the media, we have a record of executive corruption and the chance to **learn** from it. (Not that we necessarily will.)

The Watergate hearings -- more than 300 hours -- air nightly on PBS and frequently on the other networks. They are viewed, at least in part, by 85 percent of American households.

What did the President know and when did he know it?

WEICKER

BAKER

ERVIN

So now, because of the media, we have sufficient public pressure to push for the passage of laws to prevent **future** excesses. (Not that we'll necessarily enforce them.)

Senator Frank Church chairs a committee to investigate the FBI and CIA, amassing thousands of pages on phone-tapping, mail-opening, political blackmail, disruption of dissident groups, attempted murder of foreign leaders, LSD experiments on unwitting subjects...

Our society has drawn its inspiration from the biblical injunction...

ENACTED by CONGRESS
- New Permanent Committee to Renew CIA Activities
- New Secret Court to Approve Government Wiretaps
- More Public A...
- Fil...

"AND YE SHALL KNOW THE TRUTH AND THE TRUTH SHALL MAKE YOU FREE."

JOHN VIII-XXXII

The Church injunction is, incidentally, carved into a wall at the CIA in Langley, Virginia.

IN KEEPING WITH THE CURRENT NORMS OF GOVERNMENT OVERREACH,

George W. Bush offers no sedition bills after the attacks of September 11, 2001. Instead, he works behind closed doors, or through the rushed passage of bills like the Patriot Act . . .

Bypassing the court created to approve domestic eavesdropping and reinstituting Nixon-era spying . . .

- Expanding the ability of law enforcement to search telephone, e-mail, and financial records without court orders . . .
- Rolling back the Freedom of Information Act . . .
- Removing information from government websites . . .
- Classifying or reclassifying millions of documents that would have been public . . .
- Ignoring the president's statutory obligation to inform the Congress . . .
- Undermining the Watergate-era law that makes presidential records public . . .

Good question. After 9/11, a New York Times/CBS News poll showed 64 percent of Americans willing to surrender some rights to protect national security during wartime. Some 42 percent said newspapers shouldn't criticize the government.

DOES SECRECY MAKE US SAFER? CONSIDER THIS.

Are you safer not knowing if a company dumps poison in your river? In 2002, the White House classified information about critical infrastructure. Under the Homeland Security Act, if a private company voluntarily divulges relevant information to the government, that information is exempt from the Freedom of Information Act and the company is immune from prosecution. What's more, anyone who blows the whistle goes to jail.

Are you safer not knowing why we invaded Iraq? When the CIA found no decisive proof of Iraqi complicity in the 9/11 attacks or weapons of mass destruction, the White House created an "Office of Special Plans" in the Pentagon to cherry-pick the evidence, free of congressional oversight.

According to the Center for Public Integrity, the White House made 935 false statements about Iraq in the two years following the 9/11 attacks.

Barack Obama reverses Bush's policy, ordering federal agencies to presume in favor of granting freedom of information requests.

For a long time now, there's been too much secrecy in this city. That era is now over...

...To be sure, issues like personal privacy and national security must be treated with the care they demand...

...But the mere fact that you have the legal power to keep something secret does not mean you should always use it.

So he doesn't... always.

The Obama administration has decided to keep secret the locations of nearly four dozen coal-ash storage sites that pose a threat to people living nearby. It says releasing the information would compromise national security...

Top 10 States with Coal-Ash Disp

LAND-
FILL
SITES

SURFACE
IMPOUND-
MENTS
(PONDS)

A federal judge threatens to sanction the Obama administration for withholding a document from lawyers suing the government over its warrantless wiretapping program. The government has invoked the "state secrets" privilege...

So in this brief history a pattern emerges: We slip back but we recover our footing. The media expose corruption and build pressure for change -- but the **government** still has the **loudest** voice.

So when sizing up White House assertions...

Take the advice of a president who sized up **Kremlin** assertions...

Trust but verify.

...embrace this truth from one of journalism's greatest skeptics.

All governments lie.

I.F. Stone's Weekly

How the Press Is Brain-Washed and the Neutrals

...and accept that there's no free ride in democracy.

The price of freedom is eternal vigilance.

Once I gave a speech to high school students on the media coverage of the "war on terrorism," followed by a Q&A.

I want to trust my **leaders!** Why should I trust reporters? It's not their job to protect me. Why do I have to read stuff I can't do anything about?

We can **deny** our heritage and our history, but we cannot escape **responsibility** for the result.

There is no way for a citizen of a republic to **abdicate** his **responsibilities.**

Actually, Edward R. Murrow said that.

What I said was...

I know, kid. It sucks. And so much of the coverage is crap.

But if you don't inform yourself, you can't cry about how things are going.

So why **is** there so much crap? I mean, you guys are full of it!

CANIS JOURNALISTICUS

Like I haven't heard **that** before...

German philosopher Arthur Schopenhauer (1788-1860)

Journalists are like dogs -- whenever anything moves they begin to bark.

YIP YIP YIP

Norwegian playwright Henrik Ibsen (1828-1906)

It is inexcusable for scientists to torture animals. Let them make their experiments on journalists and politicians.

Irish poet William Butler Yeats (1865-1939)

I **hate** journalists. There is nothing in them but tittering, jeering emptiness. They have all made what Dante calls **"The Great Refusal."**

The shallowest people on the ridge of the Earth.

American chess Grandmaster Bobby Fischer (1943-2008)

Is it against the law to **kill** a reporter?

From 1998 to 2002, the Project for Excellence in Journalism studied minute-by-minute ratings for 154 local TV stations' newscasts, more than 30,000 stories.

It found that serious policy stories -- if done well -- were just as likely to hold viewers as car crashes. Maybe even more so.

Some say that's because competing channels and websites have siphoned off the thrill-seekers, raising the percentage of actual news junkies watching local news. Yet those shows still rely on fluff and mayhem. So maybe TV execs really don't know what those viewers like.

The polls **do** show a pretty clear picture of what most news consumers **don't** like...

The news media. Every year, fewer people **trust** them. These days, reporters who break laws to expose injustice or fraud often **lose** jury trials because jurors don't see them as advocates or checks on power.

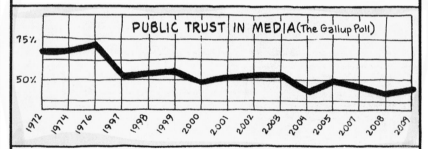

PUBLIC TRUST IN MEDIA (The Gallup Poll)

75%

50%

1972 1974 1976 1997 1998 1999 2000 2001 2002 2003 2004 2005 2007 2008 2009

Many of those verdicts are overturned on appeal, because most judges recognize the role journalism is supposed to play in our democracy. But regular people? Not so much.

They recognize us as biased, self-serving, arrogant jerks.

Why is that? Well, journalism does tend to attract a certain kind of person. Cynics. Pests. Obnoxious inquisitors. Terriers nipping at the ankles of their betters.

We never tried to win a popularity contest. We know we're not loved. Even *liked*. That doesn't matter.

The whole attitude toward us has been so cyclical. After President Nixon started his anti-media campaign, people would come up and, well, spit on you, literally. They said: **"Why don't you tell the truth!?"**

After Watergate, people came up to the press and said, **"You saved the country."**

Helen Thomas, you've covered every president since JFK. President Clinton's spokesman Mike McCurry said it was torture being grilled by you.

I'm glad to hear it! I don't **bow and scrape** to these people. True, they have a very vaunted position, but they're still our public servants. And **we, too,** are public servants. We're the only institution in our democracy that can question them on a regular basis.

So, who was the **easiest** president to cover?

None.

They're not easy, because they **think** they're **President!**

AS AUTHOR—AND JOURNALIST—ALBERT CAMUS ONCE SAID . . .

A free press can of course be good or bad, but, most certainly, without freedom it will never be anything but bad.

Do polls show declining trust in news outlets because the public thinks they're bad? Absolutely. But fluctuations in those polls suggest that appraising news coverage is not a cold calculation. It's emotional.

Take one of journalism's finest hours: Watergate. Some people are still angry about it. They say it eroded respect for our basic institutions.

What it really eroded was respect for the people in those institutions. As Haldeman observed . . .

And the implicit infallibility of presidents . . . is badly hurt by this, because it shows that people do things the President wants to do even though it's wrong, and the President can be wrong.

During the Watergate scandal, the press did what it was supposed to do. So, as Thomas noted, first it was spat on, and then it was celebrated.

When the press pulls back from doing what it's supposed to do—such as dog the White House in the run-up to war—often it is celebrated first and then spat on later.

Even if news outlets gave up pleasing audiences and advertisers and just did what they think they're supposed to do, they would still be creatures of their times.

Most of the press went along with racism when it was the norm...

Life magazine cartoon, pre-1920s.

"SAY, SAMBO, DON'T YOU THINK THIS PIECE OF WATERMELON IS RATHER LARGE?"

"GOLLY, BOSS! DAT AIN'T HALF BIG NUFF!"

Some still do.

NEW YORK POST
WEDNESDAY, FEBRUARY 18, 2009

THEY'LL HAVE TO FIND SOMEONE ELSE TO WRITE THE NEXT STIMULUS BILL

Headless Body in Topless Bar

Most (though not all) newspapers opposed women's suffrage, ignored the Nazi Holocaust, and supported the internment of Japanese-Americans during World War Two.

OUSTER OF ALL JAPS IN CALIFORNIA NEAR!
San Francisco Examiner 6¢ EXTRA
Thousands of Allies Face Japs in Java

But times change.

It's not for us today to pass judgment.... Yet we must recognize that the internment of Japanese-Americans was ... a mistake.

Mostly, reporters are celebrated or condemned not because of the importance or truth of their story, but according to whether their story suits the public's mood.

For example, the public approved of the media during Hurricane Katrina because the reporters and anchors expressed our outrage...

Excuse me, Senator ... you know, I got to tell you, there are a lot of people here who are very upset, and very angry, and very frustrated...

CNN FEDERAL RESPONSE ANDERSON COOPER 360

LOUISIANA SENATOR MARY LANDRIEU (D)

There was no water, no food, no beds, no authority there. There was no planning.

WASHINGTON, D.C.   NEW ORLEANS, LA

Dir. of Homeland Security MICHAEL CHERTOFF   MEET THE PRESS

Is there going to be help? I mean, they're very thirsty. Do you have any idea yet? Nothing? Officer?

FOX NEWS CHANNEL AMERICA'S CHALLENGE
NATIONAL GUARD TROOPS COMMENT AFTER ARRIVING IN NEW ORLEANS

...even though the coverage itself was... problematic.

They have people standing ... in that frickin' Superdome for five days watching dead bodies, watching hooligans killing people, raping people.

...One woman ... watched three men rape an eleven-year-old girl...

What a horrific thing to endure.

CNN ACTOR JIM CAVIEZEL

All kinds of reports of looting, fires and violence. Thugs shooting at rescue crews....

We have yet to confirm a lot of that.

LIVE

NEW ORLEANS IN CHAOS

There was no raped child, no 30 bodies in a Convention Center freezer. They were merely rumors repeated by officials. Later, some noted that the stories fit an ugly, if unconscious, racial narrative.

If the Dome and Convention Center had harbored large numbers of **middle-class white people**, it would not have been a fertile ground for this kind of rumor-mongering.

Times-Picayune editor Jim Amoss

The press was momentarily celebrated because its response **felt** good and true; it had what Comedy Central's mock pundit Stephen Colbert calls **"truthiness."**

The Times-Picayune

'HELP US, PLEASE'

AFTER THE DISASTER CHAOS, LAWLESSNESS RULE THE S...

The Times-Picayune

UNDER WATER

BREACH SWAMPS CITY FROM LAKE TO LE...

The Times-Picayune

La. governor seeks ne... $32 billion in hurricane a...

N.O. ...

RAPE. MURDER. GUNFIGHTS. Much of the Violence Never Happened.

Surveys find that this is deeply satisfying to news consumers.

irds on a Wire

abc **GOOD MORNING AMERICA**

Right after September 11, 2001, polls saw public trust in the media **soar.** No one much cared that rumors of toppling buildings were reported along with the real ones -- in the horror of that moment, the media **expressed our pain.**

Ah, this is terrifying -- awful.

We watch powerless. It's a horror.

But then attention shifted to the war, and the polls plunged again. Journalists scored low on morality, professionalism, and **patriotism.**

The **Hate-Bush** crowd simply will never admit anything good can come from the Iraq conflict. These people are bitter, dishonest, and of course, damaging to America.

FOX NEWS NO SPIN ZONE

Avowedly pro-war Fox News was the cable news ratings leader.

Voices favorable to the White House swamped dissenters across **all** media. On every channel, a corps of retired military men opined daily.

...there are thousands of gallons of mustard agents, Sarin nerve agent, VX, still in Iraq...

GEN. BARRY McCAFFREY (RET.)
NBC NEWS ANALYST

Later, the New York Times reported that the ubiquitous "armchair generals" were **coached** by the Pentagon, tied to war industries, or both.

Some reporters asked probing questions in the run-up to the 2002 invasion, sometimes in smaller papers, or buried inside the big ones.

DECEMBER 20, 2001

An Iraqi Defector

SEPTEMBER 8, 2002

U.S. Says Hussein

APRIL 21, 2003

Illicit Arms Kept Till

MAY 26, 2004

The Times and Iraq

Looking back, we wish we had been more aggressive in re-examining the claims as new evidence emerged — or failed to emerge.

—The Editors

cientist is d to Assert

A-Bomb Parts

den Weapons Sites

But mostly, those questions were not asked.

Courage and caution -- the **yin** and **yang** of good reporting -- fell out of balance after 9/11. People were frightened. Journalists are people. They have a survival instinct.

They love their country, and they want their country to love them.

We know we're not loved. That doesn't matter.

Speak for yourself, Helen. For most people, it matters.

NONE OF THIS IS INTENDED TO EXCUSE THE MEDIA'S PERFORMANCE.

We don't forgive surgeons who sleep on the job, or teachers who are ill-informed. We don't pardon accountants who skim a little off the top, or politicians who brazenly sell votes to the highest bidder (usually).

We expect cops to be honest and firefighters to be brave.

We expect reporters to be ethical and informed. And awake. And damn it, honest and brave.

We expect it. And yet we don't expect it.

In an article in *The Nation*, veteran *Washington Post* reporter Walter Pincus quoted something that Senator Eugene McCarthy once told him. He said the press is a bunch of blackbirds—all on a wire. One bird will fly to another wire, and when it doesn't get electrocuted, all the birds will fly to that other wire.

Congress is the safest landing strip for journalists who would challenge or criticize the White House. Congress is supposed to balance the executive branch. If our duly elected representatives complain about the President, hold a hearing on government secrecy, examine budget irregularities, or speak out on corruption, that's a story, and reporters who cover it are safe from charges of bias.

BUT SOMETIMES THAT LANDING STRIP IS BLOCKED. Back in 1971, Daniel Ellsberg first leaked the Pentagon Papers to anti-war senators, but they wouldn't touch them. In that case, the risks for newspapers were not just political, but legal.

(The prospect of litigation killed many early stories about Big Tobacco.)

But in that case, newspapers flew to the wire unprotected—a dozen of them, as one after another were slammed by injunctions—and finally brought the Vietnam War's history to light.

Capitol Hill gave questioning journalists no protective cover after the attacks of 9/11. Stonewalled by the White House, Congress clammed up. Legislators did not even demand time to review the lengthy Patriot Act, which breached basic civil liberties. They passed it, unread.

With a secretive White House and a silent Congress, news outlets were obliged, once again, to fly onto those hot wires all on their own. Mostly, they didn't.

News You *CAN'T* Use

But news consumers complain more about inaccuracy than cowardice.

More than half the people polled in a 2009 Pew study believed news stories are rife with inaccuracies. And 79 percent believed news outlets try to cover them up.

These beliefs are justified, especially the first one.

The second one isn't as true as it used to be. Once, news outlets could stonewall critics and external fact-checkers. It could take years, or forever, to set the record straight.

But nowadays, the Internet enables us to challenge and check facts instantaneously, making errors virtually impossible to cover up. So online stories note the corrections of earlier posts, ombudsmen conduct investigations, reporters engage in dialogue with their critics, and the media landscape is littered with hitherto unheard-of mea culpas.

Journalism has entered a new era of openness, all in the interest of building trust with news consumers.

Still waiting for that to work.

Hey, we all blow it once in a while. Stuff happens. Reliable sources can be wrong.

But many mistakes are born of over-confidence, flawed analysis, and the reflex to be first at the expense of being right. This happens *a lot.* Then again, it always has.

Especially when it comes to numbers.

This famous headline, printed before the votes were tallied, was based on flawed polls.

Polls.

Don't get me started.

These tracking polls were conducted the first week of **May 2008**. That week, there was something for everyone.

PRESIDENTIAL ELECTION TRACKING POLLS MAY 2008

McCAIN
OBAMA

TIMES/BLOOMBERG

USA TODAY/GALLUP

CBS

RASMUSSEN

10 20 30 40 50 60 70 80 90

A poll's precision is seductive, soothing...

...a snare and a delusion.

We need to know each pollster's methodology: how many are polled, how selected, how answers are weighed according to key demographic markers...

But just as important is the nature of the "question" itself.

If the election were held right now -- who would you vote for?

That's an irrelevant question because we aren't voting **right now.**

But pollsters ask that because if they asked the **relevant** question, even late in a campaign, maybe a third of the answers would be **this:**

Who are you voting for in **November?**

Um. I haven't decided.

News outlets pay the bill for most polling organizations. "I haven't decided" ain't news.

Polls can swing wildly when the public doesn't know or care much about the issue being polled.

But pollsters rarely ask: **How much do you care?**

Because, more often than not, we don't know or care much.

So when you catch a glimpse of a poll, avert your eyes.

Yeah. As if.

The Goldilocks Number

Once upon a time -- November 2005 -- someone said a very **scary** number...

Law enforcement officials estimate that 50,000 predators are online at any given moment! I'm Chris Hansen, reporting...

DATELINE   CHRIS HANSEN
to catch a predator

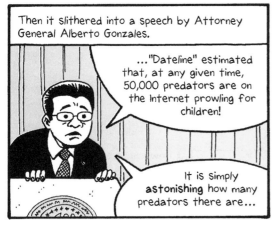

Then it slithered into a speech by Attorney General Alberto Gonzales.

..."Dateline" estimated that, at any given time, 50,000 predators are on the Internet prowling for children!

It is simply **astonishing** how many predators there are...

Maybe **too** astonishing. But tracking down that number is like following Hansel and Gretel's trail of breadcrumbs.

Let's track down NBC's Chris Hansen instead.

... So I said to Ken Lanning -- he's our expert -- I said, "Look, this number keeps surfacing. Do you think that it's reliable?" And he essentially said, "I've heard it, but depending on how you define what is a predator, it could actually be a very low estimate."

So let's track down Ken Lanning.

I couldn't confirm it. I couldn't refute it either, but I felt it was a fairly reasonable figure. Though I was **curious** about the fact that it was 50,000.

That number had popped up in the past.

In the early '80s, the number 50,000 often was used to estimate how many children were abducted by strangers each year. But research done in the early '90s found that somewhere around **200 to 300** children were abducted in this manner.

ABDUCTED CHILDREN

...then in the late '80s, there were a lot of people who were talking about satanic cults supposedly running around the country engaging in human sacrifices. And when you'd ask, well, how much of this is going on?

Once again, the **same** number popped up -- 50,000 a year!

SACRIFICED?!

Ha ha! Yes. That one was a bit more problematic -- because we **do** have good data on homicide. And at that time, there was somewhere in the neighborhood of 20,000 murders every year...

...so this meant that the satanists, all by themselves, were killing twice as many people **as all the other murderers combined.**

Reporter Carl Bialik says **50,000** took the usual path to fame: The media quote someone who may **not** know what he's talking about and...

...then they're cited to some government body, and then a study picks it up, and then the press repeats it from that study. Once it appears in the press, public officials repeat it again...

Round and round it goes.

But something Lanning said **haunted** me...

That number had popped up in the past.

Turns out -- **50,000 is a death magnet!!**

Every year 50,000 die in road accidents... and from secondhand smoke... and from trans-fats in America. Every year 50,000 die from snakebite in India... and from malaria in Asia... and from pollution in Pakistan... and from car-noise-induced heart attacks in Europe... and every day 50,000 children die from global hunger and poverty... not to mention annual human sacrifice.
What's the deal?!

Google

It wasn't a real small number ... like 200. And it wasn't a ridiculously large number ... like 10 million.

It was a *Goldilocks* number. Not too hot, not too cold.

Sometimes the simplest reasons are the scariest.

So let's chalk up most inaccuracies to sloppiness.

Let's at least assume that usually reporters don't know for sure that their facts are wrong.

A petrified man was found some time ago in the mountains south of Gravelly Ford. Every limb and feature of the stony mummy was perfect, not even excepting the left leg...

On occasion, they just lie.

Erstwhile reporter Mark Twain said that concocting amusing lies for money was nothing compared to the "clammy stillness" of the press when confronting such horrors as, say, slavery.

He called it **"the lie of silent assertion** that there wasn't anything going on in which humane and intelligent people were interested..."

Why should we help the nation lie the whole day long and then object to telling one little individual private lie in our own interest to go to bed on?

Just for the refreshment of it, I mean.

And to take the rancid taste out of our mouth.

Certainly in the bad old days of Yellow Journalism, in the screaming headlines churned out by newspaper magnates like William Randolph Hearst and Joseph Pulitzer, there was a lot of willful omission and lying.

When the USS Maine exploded in the Havana harbor on February 15, 1898, Hearst blamed Spain.

The Examiner.

THE SPIRIT OF WAR PERVADES THE BREASTS OF ALL AMERICANS.

Patriotic Citizens Advocate Recourse to Arms to Wreak Vengeance Upon Spain for the Cruel and Cowardly Destruction of the Maine.

And he continued to blame Spain, even when a U.S. naval inquiry found no evidence Spain was responsible. Hearst relished the prospect of war.

There's a famous story about an exchange of cables between Hearst and Frederic Remington, the illustrator he hired to cover Cuba in January 1897...

Everything is quiet. There is no trouble here. There will be no war. I wish to return.

Please remain. You furnish the pictures and I'll furnish the war.

Hearst's cable is cited as the ultimate proof of his cynicism. But he always denied writing it and there's no evidence he did.

In fact, the story's source, reporter James Creelman -- a known exaggerator -- was in Europe at the time.

COMING SO

CITIZEN KANE

Still, the story has stuck. It was even enacted in a movie Hearst tried to quash.

Guess he had it coming.

Hearst was genuinely outraged by Spain's ruthless treatment of its Cuban colony, where hundreds of thousands of Cubans were herded into detention camps to starve and die. He sought **justice** as well as **profits**.

There's an ongoing argument over which of those motives screws up reporting the most.

Yellow journalism -- its passions, crusades, deceit -- is still with us. In 2005, CNN's Lou Dobbs cited a statistic with biblical implications.

The invasion of illegal aliens is threatening the health of many Americans!

"Hansen's disease was so rare in America that in 40 years only 900 people were afflicted. Suddenly, in the past three years, America has more than 7,000 cases of leprosy."

CNN LOU DOBBS TONIGHT

On "60 Minutes," host Lesley Stahl confronted Dobbs with a federal report citing 7,000 cases of leprosy over the past 30 years, not three, as Dobbs claimed.

If we reported it, it's a fact.

How can you guarantee that to me?

Because ... that's the way we do business. We don't make up numbers, Lesley, do we?

Sometimes we do, Lou. The Department of Health reports that leprosy in the United States has been in sharp decline for more than 20 years.

HANSEN'S DISEASE (LEPROSY) NUMBER OF REPORTED CASES, BY YEAR — UNITED STATES, 1971-2006

Influx of refugees from Cambodia, Laos, Vietnam 1978-1988

400 360 320 280 240 200 160 120 80 40 0

1971 1976 1981 1986 1991 1996 2001 2006

Dobbs's wild exaggeration of the leprosy rate may have been an honest mistake -- until he repeated and defended it. So too, his claim that 33% of the nation's prison population was illegal immigrants. (Only 6% were.)

NO DOUBT DOBBS COULD CITE SOURCES for his jeremiads, but not *good* sources. No matter—he was immersed in visions of immigrant hordes, obsessed by doubts over Barack Obama's citizenship, convinced the U.S. government secretly planned to merge with Canada and Mexico.

Eventually, his CNN bosses said he could opine on his radio show, but had to do straight news on TV. So he quit and spoke of running for president.

Why do the media lie? In Dobbs's case: maybe he chose to believe those claims because they confirmed his fears. In Hearst's case: to sell papers and avert the deaths of countless Cubans (not sure in which order).

THE LEGENDARY BRITISH JOURNALIST CLAUD COCKBURN was on vacation in Spain in July 1936 when the Spanish army under General Francisco Franco rose up against the democratically elected Republican government.

Like many journalists, Cockburn saw the Spanish Civil War as the decisive battle between freedom and Fascism. He believed the anti-Fascist forces needed a victory to hold the world's gaze, so he invented a battle in which they triumphed over Franco's army. He lied. As for the public's *right to know?* Cockburn said:

Who **gave** them such a right? Perhaps when they have exerted themselves enough to alter the policy of their bloody government and the Fascists are beaten in Spain, they will have such a right.

This isn't an **abstract** question. It's a shocking **war.**

The Fascists won. Franco's dictatorship lasted 35 years.
Cockburn never regretted what he did to try to stop it.

The Great Refusal

Remember what W. B. Yeats said about journalists?

There is nothing in them but tittering, jeering emptiness. They have all made what Dante calls "The Great Refusal."

In his poem "Inferno," Dante tours the underworld and sees a swarm of anguished souls, barred from heaven and hell, doomed to limbo. They are the neutrals, whose lives meant nothing, because they refused to commit themselves.

... and I beheld the shade of him, who made through cowardice the Great Refusal.

Robert Kennedy said that President John Kennedy's favorite quote was from "Inferno," about the Great Refusal.

The hottest places in hell are reserved for those who in time of moral crisis preserve their neutrality.

Close enough.

On the other hand, an important poem penned in the devastating wake of the First World War and the Bolshevik revolution fervently asserts: Deeply held conviction leads to mayhem.

Turning and turning in the widening gyre
The falcon cannot hear the falconer...

"Things fall apart; the centre cannot hold;
Mere anarchy is loosed upon the world,
The blood-dimmed tide is loosed, and everywhere
The ceremony of innocence is drowned..."

The **best** lack all conviction, while the **worst**
Are full of passionate intensity.

Damn you, Yeats! Pick a side!

Yeats is the typical news consumer. On any issue -- where one person sees moral courage, another sees culpable bias.

Bias v. conviction

In a 2009 poll, 60% of respondents charged news organizations with bias, up from 45% in 1985. In both years, they saw a mostly liberal bias.

And in fact, reporters are more likely than the general public to identify themselves as liberal.

U.S.S. BIAS

In 2006, New York Times publisher Arthur Sulzberger, Jr., spoke to graduates at the State University of New York at New Paltz.

It wasn't supposed to be this way.

You weren't supposed to be graduating into a world where we are still fighting for fundamental human rights, whether it's the rights of immigrants to start a new life, or the rights of gays to marry, or the rights of women to choose.

You weren't supposed to be graduating into a world where oil still drove policy and environmentalists have to fight relentlessly for every gain. You weren't, but you are. And for that, I'm sorry.

I must be honest. I can only read so many paragraphs of a New York Times story before I puke.

STATE UNIVERSITY OF NEW YORK
NEW PALTZ

It appears that Sulzberger is a liberal. Is his newspaper liberal?

MOST AMERICANS DON'T READ THE *TIMES*, but among those who express an opinion, Republicans disapprove of the paper by a margin of nearly two to one, while Democrats favor it almost five to one.

A 2002 study by Jim Kuypers at Virginia Tech examined 116 newspapers, including the *Times*. He concluded that the print press operates within a narrow range of mostly liberal beliefs. Those on the far left are ignored, and those who hold what he defines as moderate or conservative views are either denigrated or labeled as "minority opinions."

And yet liberal media watchdogs have found that the mainstream media quote far more conservatives than liberals. They have polled reporters and found them liberal on social issues but conservative on economic ones. And they note that "he who pays the piper calls the tune," and the media's paymasters are a handful of multinational corporations—hardly bastions of liberalism.

So do liberal reporters report liberally, or don't they?

The Center for Media and Public Affairs at George Mason University surveyed ABC, NBC, and CBS's evening news coverage of Presidents Ronald Reagan, Bill Clinton, and George W. Bush during their first seven months in office. Then they analyzed the coverage of President Barack Obama from Inauguration Day through December 31, 2009.

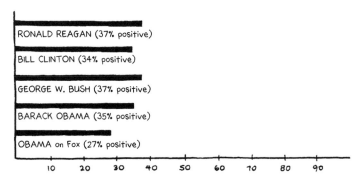

Conclusive proof: the media are biased against presidents!

The argument over political bias is one that anyone can win. It's boring.

Sure, the media are beset by biases, but they're probably not what you think.

Here are the biases *I* think you should worry about . . .

COMMERCIAL BIAS

The biggest bias. News needs conflict and momentum. It needs to be **new.** That's why news outlets too rarely follow up on stories they've already reported. We crave novelty. Like George Eliot said...

We do not expect people to be deeply moved by what is not unusual.

If we had a keen vision and feeling of all ordinary human life, it would be like hearing the grass grow and the squirrel's heart beat, and we should die of that roar which lies on the other side of silence.

As it is, the quickest of us walk about well wadded with stupidity.

Now in the third hour of the high-speed car chase...

LIVE

BREAKING NEWS
UNIVERSAL CITY

4

BAD NEWS BIAS

We are wired to care about anything that even remotely threatens us -- so emphasizing bad news is good business.

This makes the world seem more dangerous than it actually is.

STATUS QUO BIAS

This is a term that refers to our preference, all other things being equal, for things to **stay the same.**

Human beings tend to oppose change unless the benefits are guaranteed to be huge -- and the risks minuscule.

Because of the status quo bias, the media ignore any position that advocates radical change.

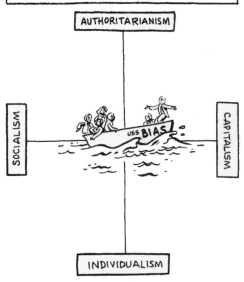

AUTHORITARIANISM

SOCIALISM

CAPITALISM

USS BIAS

INDIVIDUALISM

Andrew Cline's Rhetorica Network offers an incisive breakdown of bias. For instance, he says...

The status quo bias is expressed in the belief that "the system works." Even when covering the Florida election fiasco in 2000...

U.S.S. **BIAS**

"The mainstream media never question the **structure** of the political system. The American way is the **only** way, politically and socially..."

"This bias ensures that **alternate** points of view about how government might run and what government might do are effectively **ignored.**"

ACCESS BIAS

Reporters believe they must patrol the halls of power, but the price of admission is steep. Antagonize power and the door is barred. So sometimes journalists dance with the devil.

Whenever reporters quote a "senior administration official," they've allowed their source to hide. But if we don't know *who* is speaking, we can't ascertain *why*. We can be more easily manipulated. See if the blind quote is worth it. Usually it isn't.

The problem, of course, is that when journalists are held captive by their sources, they are susceptible to Stockholm syndrome. They empathize with their jailers.

After all, when you're fed an exclusive quote, it's natural to be grateful.

When you're man-hugged by the powerful at any one of the half-dozen black tie parties the Washington press throws for politicians each year, it's natural to be flattered.

Reporters treated John McCain and George W. Bush relatively kindly during their first presidential campaigns, partly because they seemed to *like* reporters. As the *New York Times* noted at the time, Bush "not only slaps reporters' backs but also rubs the tops of their heads and, in a few instances, pinches their cheeks."

Obviously, the biggest risk for access-dependent journalists is self-censorship.

Former CNN news chief Eason Jordan said CNN did not cover stories of brutal suppression in Saddam's Iraq for years in order to protect his Baghdad bureau and staff. At least one known CNN source died gruesomely, despite Jordan's efforts. So why maintain a bureau you can't effectively use?

Legendary Washington reporter I. F. Stone famously shunned off-the-record events. Instead, he pored over government documents other reporters ignored, scooping them with stories hidden in plain sight.

But that is extremely unglamorous work in a glamorous town, where reporters often are more glamorous than the people they cover.

VISUAL BIAS

News that has a visual hook is more likely to be noticed.

For instance, the Washington Post ran the first front-page story about the torture of detainees three months **before** the Iraq war began.

The Washington Post
DECEMBER 26, 2002
U.S. Decries Abuse but Defends Interrogations
'Stress and Duress' Tactics Used on Terrorism Suspects Held in Secret Overseas Facilities
By DANA PRIEST and BARTON GELLMAN

Press accounts of torture appeared sporadically through 2003 into 2004.

But it wasn't until April 28, 2004, that anyone, even much of the media, noticed. Pictures made us notice.

60 MINUTES

NARRATIVE BIAS

My favorite bias. Who doesn't love a good story? But stories have beginnings, middles, and ends. Some news stories, science stories for instance, never really end. **They're all middle.** It's a narrative nightmare.

Try to fix the problem by tacking on a provisional ending, and the reports appear more conclusive than they really are. So we see strings of stories like this...

JULY 7
FAT MAKES YOU FAT!

JULY 8
FAT MAKES YOU THIN!

JULY 9
CHOCOLATE GIVES YOU ACNE!

JULY 10
CHOCOLATE WON'T GIVE YOU ACNE!

JULY 11
CHOCOLATE HELPS YOUR HEART!

JULY 12
ONLY THE EXPENSIVE KIND!

The great thing about a narrative is that once a template is set with plots and characters, it can be reused again and again when reporting on the same subject, as during presidential campaigns.

FRAT BOY

MENDACIOUS PRIG

Standard plot for election coverage: Who's winning the horse race. Standard subplot: How reporters fail the public by obsessing on the horse race.

EFFETE FRANCOPHILE

SCHEMING EMASCULATOR

SAVIOR

The characters, obviously, change with the years.

Pat Robertson and Jerry Falwell ... [are] agents of intolerance ...

I don't think [the NRA] help the Republican Party at all...

Our party's pro-life plank should be changed to allow exceptions for rape, incest, or to save the life of the mother...

McCAIN 2000 STRAIGHT TALK EXPRESS — ★ —

But sometimes, when, say, an erstwhile media darling changes his narrative, reporters are forced to rewrite the script. This can be very annoying.

McCAIN 2008

I don't believe those things anymore.

His idea was nixed, but he did give a rope and sledgehammer to the Iraqis entering the square.

The media, based in a nearby hotel, streamed out to watch their fruitless efforts.

Because of the media, the Marines were called in. One draped Saddam's face in an American flag --

-- which was hastily removed.

We didn't want to look like an occupation force.

The media, egged on by their editors at home, zoomed in to make the sparse crowd look bigger, signaling the war's end in a swift and unambiguous blaze of glory.

That day cable news focused the world's attention on the thrilling video. Fox News replayed it every 4.4 minutes. CNN replayed it every 7.7 minutes. Even then, they could have used a wider angle and shown the square in its proper context.

They **could** have used a wider shot -- but the pictures wouldn't have fit the narrative.

FAIRNESS BIAS

Journalists will bend over backward to appear balanced by offering equal time to opposing viewpoints, even when they aren't equal. Often they bend to the right, to evade the charge of liberal bias.

USA TODAY

AUGUST 19, 2004 Newsline

Fog of War, Partisanship, Cloud Kerry's War Record

A clear picture of what John Kerry did or did not do in Vietnam 35 years ago may never emerge

Case in point: the "Swift Boat Veterans for Truth." The group, funded by a major Republican campaign donor, launched a series of attacks against Democratic presidential candidate John Kerry. It claimed in ads that Kerry lied to get one of his two decorations for bravery and two of his three Purple Hearts for service in Vietnam.

The charges blanketed talk radio, and were repeated hundreds of times on network TV and in newspapers. The Swift Boat ads were awarded a fortune in free TV time as the mainstream media chewed over the controversy.

The charges were quickly debunked by Navy records and Kerry's crewmates—but the reporting on the actual evidence was drowned in a miasma of mainstream media weasel-speak, the surest sign of terminal fairness bias.

If the substance of many of the charges ... aren't holding up ... why is it resonating so much?

NBC's Tim Russert should have known why. In a textbook example of fairness bias, for weeks the mainstream media flooded the zone with "equal coverage" of the two unequal sides, distorting the truth in pursuit of the appearance of balance.

It might seem that fairness bias *looms largest* on the political beat. But ultimately **all** stories are political.

That's why the editors of Scientific American published this snarky response to its critics on April Fool's Day, 2005.

In retrospect, this magazine's coverage of so-called evolution has been hideously one-sided.

JOHN RENNIE, Editor

For decades, we published articles in every issue that endorsed the ideas of Charles Darwin and his cronies.

ON THE ORIGINS OF SPECIES C. DARWIN

True, the theory of common descent through natural selection has been called **the unifying concept for all of biology and one of the greatest scientific ideas of all time**, but that was no excuse to be fanatics about it.

Good journalism values balance above all else. We owe it to our readers to present everybody's ideas equally and not to ignore or discredit theories simply because they lack scientifically credible arguments or facts.

Nor should we succumb to the easy mistake of thinking that scientists understand their fields better than, say, U.S. Senators or best-selling novelists do.

JURASSIC PARK CRICHTON
STATE of FEAR
SPHERE
CONGO Chrichton
AIRFRAME
TIMELINE
CRICHTON

Indeed, if politicians or special interest groups say things that seem untrue or misleading, our duty as journalists is to quote them without comment or contradiction.

To do otherwise would be elitist and therefore wrong.

JOHN RENNIE, Editor

WAR

"... all action takes place ... in a kind of twilight, which, like fog or moonlight, often tends to make things seem grotesque and larger than they really are ...

"Whatever is hidden from full view in this feeble light ... has to be guessed at by talent or simply left to chance."

—Carl Philipp Gottlieb von Clausewitz (1780–1831), soldier and military theorist

EVERY MEDIA BIAS SHOWS UP in war reporting, in spades.

Commercial bias? Nowhere is context sacrificed more for action than in war stories: the daily battle, car bomb, drone attack, beheading.

Status quo bias is elevated as a matter of patriotism. Reporters don't wantonly attack leaders when the nation is at risk. (And *any* attack seems wanton.)

Access bias? The military can bar, expel, and jail reporters. It can also—this goes without saying—save their lives. Without friends in uniform, war reporters are more at risk.

Visual bias grows with every new technological advance, from battlefield sketches to satellite feeds to amateur cell phone video.

As for *bad news bias*—well, that's the whole story of war.

Narrative bias comes into play long before the shooting starts. Government supplies the plot, the threat, and the enemy's depravity. Atrocity stories are recycled from war to war. Like killing babies.

They took the babies out of the incubator, took the incubators, and left the babies to **die** on the cold floor.

YOUNG NAYIRAH TESTIFIED in October 1990 before some members of Congress that Iraqi soldiers invaded the hospital in Kuwait City where she was a volunteer. Viewers were told her full name was being withheld to protect her family, still in occupied Kuwait.

In fact, she was Nayirah al-Sabah, daughter of the Kuwaiti ambassador to the U.S. The atrocity was a fiction, crafted with the help of public relations giant Hill & Knowlton.

In January 1991, a bare majority of 52 senators voted for the resolution to go to war. Some believe the incubator story made the difference.

Whether dead babies, the sinking of the *Maine* and the *Lusitania*, the attacks in the Gulf of Tonkin, or Saddam Hussein's weapons of mass destruction, the premises for going to war usually are built on partial or total fabrications. Fundamentally, this is because our government does not trust us to come to the right conclusion—that is, *to go to war.*

The best defense against deception is more reporting, but, as we've seen, journalists often swallow the fabrications whole.

You may have noticed that I haven't mentioned the fairness bias. It doesn't get much of a workout during war. Ex–war reporter Chris Hedges wrote that war reporters become addicted to the rush of battle. And even when staring mayhem in the mouth, they may distort what they see.

"For they . . . also embrace the cause. They may do it with more skepticism. They certainly expose more lies and misconceptions. But they believe. We all believe."

Combat reporters focus on the fighting. The reason, *our reason* for fighting, is lost in the fog of war. And once that's lost, it takes a long, long time to recover.

In 1854, London Times reporter William Howard Russell reports on the charge of the British Light Cavalry Brigade in Crimea.

At ten minutes past 11 ... they swept proudly past, glittering in the morning sun in all the pride and splendor of war...

... At 35 minutes past 11, not a single British soldier except the **dead** and the **dying** was left in front of the Muscovite guns.

He writes of soldiers ill-fed, ill-led, wounded, and left on the field to die.

Prince Albert is furious.

That miserable scribbler!!

Russell's reporting turns the public against the government, prompting history's **first** order of military censorship.

Henceforth, any reporter who reports information that could be useful to the enemy will be **expelled**.

Russell is hailed as "the father of war reporting." Not exactly, he says.

I am the **miserable** parent of a **luckless** tribe.

A few years later he covers the American Civil War, until his press credentials are yanked.

The Civil War is the first to be widely photographed **and** telegraphed. In 1844, Samuel Morse debuted his device by sending this:

– ··· – ·· · ·–· · ·–· ··· ·– *

·–· ·· – – –·· ––·

·–· ·–· –· –· ·–· –·· ·–· – *

*WHAT HATH GOD WROUGHT?

Interesting question.

The immediacy of the new technology fires an insatiable appetite for battlefield drama.

Telegraph fully all news you can get and when there is no news, **send rumors.**

Some revel in the telegraph. Others shudder at the **chaos** it unleashes.

It covers us all over with **lies**, fills the very air we breathe and obscures the very sun; makes us **doubt** of everything we read, because we know that the chances are ten to one it is **false...**

Sounds familiar.

HARPER'S WEEKLY.

A JOURNAL OF CIVILIZATION.

[Vol VII – No. 357.] New York, Saturday, October 31, 1863.

...00 Per Year in Advance. Single Copies Six Cents.

E... ...Congress, in the Year 1863, by Harper & Brothers, in the Clerk's Office of the District Court.

After Theodore R. Davis

THE ARMY OF THE CUMBERLAND. REBEL ATTACK UPON WAGONS IN ANDERSON GAP

Sketched by Mr. THEODORE R. DAVIS

THE ARMY OF THE CUMBERLAND

WE devote pages 689, 692, 696, and 697 to illustrations of the Army of the Cumberland. On pages 696 and 697 will be found a fine battle scene, which will convey an idea of the gallant stand made by General Thomas's heroes against the rebel advance at the battle of Chicamauga, when they saved the day and covered themselves and their leader with glory.

On pages 689 and 692 we reproduce three illustrations of the cavalry operations which followed the battle, from sketches by Mr. Theodore R. Davis, who writes:

HEAD-QUARTERS MAJOR-GENERAL GRANGER, CHATTA-NOOGA, October 7, 1863.

Arriving at Bridgeport during a pelting rain-storm, and at night, I domiciled until morning under a railroad platform that seemed to comprise the town.

The morning came, and out I crawled, finding, after much in-quiry, that "the way to reach Chattanooga was to walk, of course;" and "the distance by the safe route was only sixty miles." "But," quoth my informant, "General Wheeler, with all the cavalry of Bragg's army, is on that route now." My bunk-mates of the pre-

[cont'd on p. 689]

General William T. Sherman, appalled by this army of ink-stained wretches, bans them from the front -- but would gladly march them to the **sea**.

I regard them as **spies**, which in truth, they are.

Reporters lie. They leak secret war plans. They expose tragic blunders. So War Secretary Edwin Stanton adds two new weapons to his arsenal: the **press pass** and the **press release**.

So now we're barred from the front, and our papers print press releases from the Army instead. Unedited!

Plus, Stanton controls all the telegraph lines.

And he imposes a news blackout. Hysterical rumors fill the void.

Cut off from supplies, Southern newspapers print on wallpaper. Northern editors abuse each other in print and bash Lincoln's war strategy. New York Tribune editor Horace Greeley is a **raving** armchair general.

HARPER'S WEEKLY, March 29, 1862

Some even claim his abolitionist war fever affected the Union generals, whose bad planning led to defeat at Bull Run.

But the Tribune redeems itself at Antietam...

September 17, 1862, the **bloodiest** day in U.S. history. Tribune reporter George Smalley quietly attaches himself to General Joe Hooker's staff.

Fierce and desperate battle between 200,000 men has raged since daylight...

...Pale and bloody faces are everywhere upturned. They are sad and terrible...

He is not "impartial" -- no one is -- but he's honest, courageous, and clear. His account is a paragon of American war journalism.

After Kurz & Allison.

Smalley presses a telegraph operator to send a dispatch to his New York editors. Instead, it's transmitted directly to Lincoln, desperately awaiting word.

The enemy's batteries ... were fortunately either partially disabled or short of ammunition ... I believe it is the prelude to a victory tomorrow.

TAP TAP TAP

Smalley assumes that tomorrow, General George McClellan will fight on. He doesn't.

Lincoln fires McClellan.

Out of the Civil War emerges the template for future war journalism -- use and abuse of new technology, press releases, censorship, passive reporting...

Reporting of dazzling clarity, and reporting warped in the heat of high ideals and love of country.

Oh, and something else comes out of the Civil War...

ANTIETAM
NATIONAL BATTLEFIELD
NATIONAL PARK SERVICE
U.S. DEPARTMENT OF THE INTERIOR

Bylines!

Before the war, reporting is anonymous.

The founding fathers used pseudonyms to attack each other in print.

But General Joe Hooker, enraged by the press, demands reporters sign their work. Then they can...

... abuse or criticize me to their hearts' content!

In future wars, the military contains the media through the skillful deployment of carrots and sticks, and an irresistible force -- **patriotism**.

It's said that Senator Hiram Johnson, opposing America's entry into World War One in 1917, first uttered the words that have resounded ever since...

The first casualty, when war comes, is **truth**.

In his 1916 campaign, Woodrow Wilson had run **against** entry into the war -- in 1917 he wants to **sell** it. So he outlaws dissent (with the Espionage and Sedition Acts) and builds a powerful propaganda machine.

The world must be made safe for democracy.

His new Committee on Public Information (CPI) spreads war fever by suppressing bad news, equating dissent with disloyalty -- and demonizing the enemy.

Master Production

The KAISER
"The beast of Berlin"
An Amazing Exposé of the Intimate Life of the Mad Dog of Europe

Once lead this People into war and they will forget there ever was such a thing as **tolerance.**

Suddenly, merely having a German last name can be dangerous.

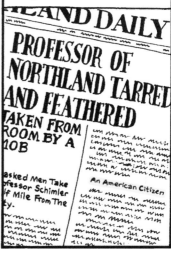

...LAND DAILY

PROFESSOR OF NORTHLAND TARRED AND FEATHERED

TAKEN FROM ROOM BY A MOB

asked Men Take ofessor Schimler If Mile From The ty.

An American Citizen

CPI chief George Creel says that on any given week, more than 20,000 newspaper columns are filled with CPI material -- material that is...

...not propaganda as the Germans defined it -- but propaganda in the **true** sense of the word, meaning the **"propagation of faith."**

PERSHING'S CRUSADERS

79

France and Britain bar most reporters from the front. In 1916, the United Press's George Seldes is one of several restless Americans reporting from London.

Of the first war years I will say just this: I made a total fool of myself when I accepted as true the news reports from New York and Europe which by their volume and repetition overwhelmed what little **objective** intelligence I had.

I used all the stories of German atrocities, including the Baltimore preacher's "unimpeachable" account of the crucifixion of Canadian soldiers by the enemy.*

*No evidence of the claim is ever found.

During the entire 19 months of American involvement in World War One, the government prohibits any photos of American dead.

We were shown nothing of the **realities** of the war ... We were, in short, merely part of the great Allied propaganda machine whose purpose was to sustain morale at all costs and help drag unwilling America into the slaughter.

...We all more or less lied about the war.

As the war ends, a few reporters slip into Germany. Seldes interviews German Supreme Army Commander Paul von Hindenburg.

The American infantry in the Argonne won the war. The day came ... when ... there was nothing left to do but ask terms.

General Pershing censors the interview -- and then **court-martials** Seldes and the other reporters for crossing into Germany in violation of the Armistice.

The Germans suffer horribly after the war. Many blame their military defeat on the sabotage of German socialists, Communists, and Jews. The Nazis call it the "stab in the back." It's a **very popular** idea.

Even the influential Paul von Hindenburg cites it. Why not? No one knows that he once admitted Germany lost to superior force on the battlefield.

If the ... interview had been passed by Pershing's censors at the time, it would have been headlined in every country civilized enough to have newspapers, and ... made an impression on millions of people...

I believe it would have destroyed the main planks on which **Hitler** rose to power ... and it would have changed the future of all mankind.

Many journalists are embedded with the troops. The legendary Ernie Pyle writes columns on their grinding ordeal and uncomplicated courage.

...Every line and sag of their bodies speaks their inhuman exhaustion...

In their eyes as they pass is not hatred, not excitement, not despair ... Just the simple expression of being here as though they had been here doing this forever, and nothing else.

Pyle is killed by Japanese machine-gun fire in 1945, one of few civilians awarded a Purple Heart. His final column is found in his pocket.

There are many of the living who have had burned into their brains forever the unnatural sight of cold dead men ... Dead men in such monstrous infinity that you come almost to hate them.

The information is controlled: casualty figures are fudged and losses redefined as wins. Still, mixed messages slip through. **Except** when the atomic bomb drops on August 6, 1945. The White House controls **that** story entirely...

"The Japanese began the war from the air at Pearl Harbor. They have been repaid many fold..."

"Sixteen hours ago an American airplane dropped one bomb on Hiroshima, an important Japanese Army base..."

"It is an atomic bomb ... a harnessing of the basic power of the universe."

As Robert Lifton and Greg Mitchell note 50 years later, that first official statement begins with a half-truth: Hiroshima does contain an important military base -- but the bomb is dropped in the very center of the city.

It is U.S. policy to bomb Japanese civilian centers to undermine morale.

The government is gratified that often the media print the official press releases in their entirety...

CHICAGO DAILY NEWS

U.S. Hurls Secret Weapon

ATOM BOMBS DOOM JAPS

Steel Tower Vanishes in Smoke in Test

SHORTENS WAR, STIMSON SAYS

Power Beyond Belief

Flash Outdoes Daylight

Truman Bares Earth-Shaker

...releases frequently written by New York Times reporter William "Atomic Bill" Laurence, long-time A-bomb advocate, now on the Pentagon payroll.

Laurence is never on the ground in Japan...

...but he is on the plane that drops the bomb on Nagasaki.

Awe-struck, we watched it shoot upward ... like a meteor coming from the earth ... a new species of being, born right before our incredulous eyes.

Laurence wins a Pulitzer Prize for his extensive reporting on the atomic bomb. But he gives short shrift to its lethal new feature: **radiation.**

In the immediate aftermath, reporters are barred from Hiroshima and Nagasaki -- but welcomed on the USS Missouri, to witness the Japanese surrender on September 2, 1945.

Meanwhile, Australian journalist Wilfred Burchett slips into Hiroshima for a single day...

I write these facts as dispassionately as I can in the hope that they will act as a warning to the world.

Many people had suffered only a slight cut ... They should have recovered quickly. But they did not ... Their gums began to bleed and then they vomited blood. And finally they died.

All ... they told me ... due to the radioactivity released by the atomic bomb's explosion of the uranium atom.

DAILY EXPRESS
THE ATOMIC PLAGUE
"I write this as a warning to the world!"
DOCTORS FALL AS THEY WORK

Hiroshima Simply Gone

The offical position is that the bomb released no lethal radiation. Reports to the contrary are suppressed both in the U.S. and Japan.

In the New York Times, William Laurence parrots the government.

The Japanese are still continuing their propaganda, aimed at creating ... sympathy for themselves ... The Japanese described symptoms that did not ring true.

Chicago Daily News reporter George Weller sneaks into bomb-flattened Nagasaki by passing himself off as a U.S. colonel. All of his dispatches are intercepted and destroyed by General MacArthur's censors.

All censored information is fundamentally propaganda...

Years later, he says that every event has a moment when it can be understood politically. But if that moment is missed...

...the possibility of comprehension will never return again.

"The aim of well-timed censorship is to instill this simple idea:

"It probably never happened."

In August 1946, The New Yorker magazine devoted an entire issue to a single article by journalist John Hersey -- **"Hiroshima."** It sold out within hours.

THE NEW YORKER

A REPORTER AT LARGE

HIROSHIMA

I-A NOISELESS FLASH

The entire text -- 31,000 words -- was broadcast in the U.S. and elsewhere.

... the burns had made patterns -- of undershirt straps and suspenders and on the skin of some women ... the shapes of flowers they had had on their kimonos.

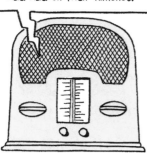

John Hersey...

What has kept the world safe from the bomb since 1945 has not been deterrence, in the sense of fear of specific weapons, so much as it's been **memory.**

The memory of what happened at Hiroshima.

For much of the '60s, journalists move freely in Vietnam. As in World War Two, media and military are **united** in a common cause.

The narrative focuses on images of brave boys, fighting for nothing less than the American way of life. A few newspapers question war policy -- but this is the **living room war**.

TV reporters attend daily briefings before trolling for **footage** to feed network combat cravings, but actual **gore** is rarely shown. Too disturbing.

DanRather - Vietnam LIVE

Sometimes, however, unexpected **static** disrupts the storyline.

In 1965, Morley Safer follows some Marines to the village of Cam Ne. They order the villagers to evacuate -- then torch their huts with flame-throwers and Zippo lighters.

That doesn't fit the narrative. That makes many people angry.

One of them calls CBS President Frank Stanton.

Frank, are you trying to fuck me!?!

Who is this?

Frank, this is your **president**...

... and yesterday your boys **shat** on the **American flag**.

In January 1968, some 70,000 North Vietnamese regulars and guerrillas launch a coordinated attack on the South during the lunar new year, Tet.

They suffer staggering losses and are soundly defeated.

Actually, in nearly **every** battle of the war, the North Vietnamese are soundly defeated.

Yet many believe the Tet offensive soured America on the war. They blame the media for spinning the **victory** of Tet into political **defeat**.

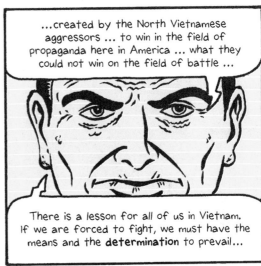

"VIETNAM SYNDROME" is one enduring phrase from the Vietnam War. "Credibility gap" is another.

In the early 1960s, reporters did not question the policy behind the war. At most, they dissented on tactics. But as the conflict dragged on, the daily briefings in Saigon, known as the Five O'Clock Follies, increasingly contradicted what the war reporters could see for themselves.

They duly quoted government assertions that the South Vietnamese army was effective and the campaign to win the peasants' hearts and minds was succeeding, but they could see that neither was true. Eventually, they had to confront the fact that *reality* had an inescapable anti-war bias. So they rejected the official progress reports and reported what they saw, but *that* did not turn the public against the war. So what did?

Americans grow weary when the human cost of combat rises. William Hammond of the Army's Office of Military History cites a Gallup Poll that found that every time the number of Americans killed and wounded increased by a factor of ten—from 1,000 to 10,000 to 100,000—public support dropped 15 points.

After Tet, Cronkite suggested that when an enemy can absorb defeat after defeat, yet continue to grow in number, "winning" is meaningless. But by the time he uttered the loaded word *stalemate*, the public's confidence in the White House had long begun its slide.

Hammond wrote that it wasn't the *press*, but flawed strategy, bad intelligence—*the war itself*—that alienated the American public in the end.

President Johnson refused to see it, until Cronkite *said* it on the evening news.

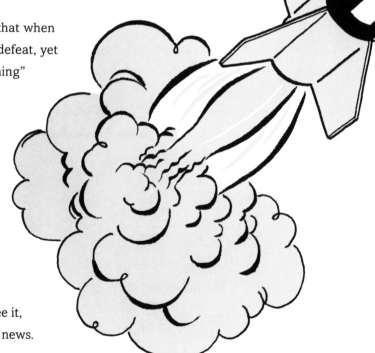

IN EARLY 1991, GEORGE BUSH SENIOR was seeking support to send a half million troops against the Iraqi invasion force in Kuwait. He warned that America had fought in Vietnam with "one hand tied behind their back." And 79 percent of Americans *agreed*, according to a study conducted soon after by the University of Massachusetts, Amherst.

When they were asked how many *Vietnamese* died in that war, their median guess was around 100,000—just one-twentieth of the actual toll of nearly two million.

"The devastation inflicted upon the Vietnamese has been shrunk," the researchers concluded, "so that it fits more easily with the image of an irresolute, half-hearted military campaign, made impotent by the objections of the anti-war movement."

Reagan's view had prevailed. Most Americans backed the Pentagon's decision to bridle the media.

In 1990–91, during the 30-day air war and four-day ground war against Iraq, the media attended daily briefings filled with maps, high-tech videos, and not one word assessing civilian casualties. The emphasis was on the smart bombs—the "bang-bang."

Selected reporters were escorted to the battlefield in "pools," to write dispatches for the rest of the media. Their reports, reviewed by the authorities for security breaches, often were delayed until they were no longer "news."

Detroit Free Press reporter Frank Bruni saw his description of pilots changed from "giddy" to "proud." Not sure what the *security* concern was there.

Meanwhile, television rang with ecstatic appraisals of what truly *was* a very efficient war.

Viewers heard from many retired generals, but very few dissenting views.

In fact, that Amherst study found that the more people watched TV, the *less* they knew about the history of the conflict, the politics, or the region.

"The only fact that did not fit in with this pattern was the ability to identify the Patriot missile," the researchers wrote. "This is a sad indictment of television's priorities."

But without field reporters, some military triumphs went largely unreported. So the Pentagon -- gearing up for the 2003 Iraq War -- abruptly changed course: Reporters now would be **embedded** with the troops.

But the **rules** were **strict.** Journalists who left their assigned units to cover anything else would not be allowed to return. And, of course, **some** information could not be reported.

The Pentagon's goal was to build trust and admiration for the military.

And despite some reporting on civilian deaths -- never shown on TV -- the embeds' narrative was of brave soldiers risking their lives to save our lives, and sometimes, the **reporters'** lives. The embeds' vision was limited.

They could see where the missiles were **launched** -- not where they **landed.**

Slate "Pressbox" columnist Jack Shafer observed...

The Pentagon officer who conceived the embedded-journalist program should step forward and demand a **fourth** star for his epaulets!

By prepping reporters in boot camps and then throwing them in harm's way with the invading force, the U.S. military has generated a bounty of positive coverage of the Iraq invasion...

...one that decades of spinning, bobbing, and weaving at rear-echelon briefings could never achieve.

blah, numbers, numbers, blah...

Over the first six weeks of "major combat operations" in Iraq, NPR's embedded reporter John Burnett checked in weekly with my show, "On the Media."

He's a very smart guy -- he knew his view would be limited, but he also saw it as a rare opportunity. Which in fact, it was.

Burnett said **this** after three days in the field...

... We've met the chief of staff, we've met the assistant commander. They've all said, "What can we do to help you do your job?" ... Not something you would expect...

So I'm encouraged so far.

Burnett said this after **three weeks** in the field...

It's the same old Pentagon routine of just telling you as much as they want to tell you and not telling you any more.

We've just moved the entire press conference into a combat zone. So yes, it has gotten very **frustrating**...

Burnett told me this, after he had left the unit to report on his own...

Just by happenstance, I stopped into a small village, Al-Taniya ... bombed by the U.S. Air Force.

Thirty men, women, and children were killed in their beds as they slept.

The U.S. Air Force says that they were precision-guided bombs aimed at tanks and track vehicles and they all struck their targets, and they really had no explanation...

...Now, embeds couldn't see that.

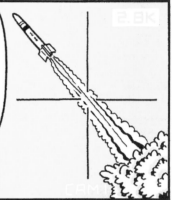

My eleven-year-old son got a G.I. Joe that was an Ernie Pyle doll, for Christmas.

And I kind of marveled at that, you know ... war correspondent as hero ... Certainly, there will be no wars again, like World War Two, when there was a unanimity of the righteousness of the cause.

"I just -- I wonder if there are going to be any Ernie Pyles again?"

Ernie Pyle

△ CAUTION △ WARNING

94

Michael Herr was 27 when he covered Vietnam for Esquire in 1967. Ten years later, he published a profound and graphic depiction of the war.

DISPATCHES

Michael Herr

The grunts were often warm, but sometimes he felt impersonal hatred, as one might hate a parasite...

They only hated me ... the way you'd hate any hopeless fool who would put himself through this thing when he had choices ... Any fool who had no more need of his life than to play with it in this way.

Once he overhears a rifleman airing that disgust in vivid terms...

Those fucking guys ... I hope they die.

PRESS

But Herr said reporters also feared a different kind of death...

We all knew that if you stayed too long you became one of those poor bastards who had to have a war on all the time ... I didn't know -- it took the war to teach it -- that you were as responsible for everything you **saw** as you were for everything you **did.**

To well and truly report a war -- amidst official lies, commercial pressures, horror, trauma, principles, and patriotism -- is to be at war with oneself. Objectivity is essential.

Objectivity is impossible.

OBJECTIVITY

Objectivity emerges as a selling point in American journalism...

When the price of a newspaper drops to a penny.

When newspapers cost six cents, nearly all of their funding came from deep-pocketed political parties and a few thousand well-heeled subscribers.

The Cape Cod Republican

Greene Co. Whig.

But in 1833, the New York Sun tries a new business model: slash the price to sell on the street to immigrants and workers, multiply the readership -- then deliver that readership to eager advertisers, who make the papers profitable.

ATLANTIC CROSSED
IN
THREE DAYS!
SIGNAL TRIUMPH
OF
MR. MONCK MASON'S
FLYING
MACHINE !!!

THE MODEL.

OF THE VI...

The content changes, too: more local politics, more crime, more drama, more scoops. **News** is a commodity like bread. **Freshness matters. Inaccuracy** -- like this balloon hoax, penned by Edgar Allan Poe -- **doesn't.**

Readership **soars.**

As always, technology facilitates the revolution. New rotary presses keep adding capacity, flooding the streets with cheap newsprint.

This is when modern journalism begins.

Ads make the penny-paper magnates **rich**. And they defend them **all**...

...by arguing that the ad revenue ensures their **political independence**.

The Sun's motto promises its working class readers **"all the news."** But of course, one man's news is another man's **blah-blah-blah.**

"The proceedings of Congress thus far would not interest our readers."

Impartiality becomes a selling point, but it's equally hard to pin down. That's why New York Herald publisher James Gordon Bennett can proclaim...

We shall support no party ... and care nothing for any candidate... We shall endeavor to record facts ... stripped of verbiage and coloring...

...and yet go on in the Herald to colorfully paint such candidates as Republican presidential nominee Abraham Lincoln as...

...a **fourth-rate** lecturer who cannot speak good grammar ... delivers his **hackneyed, illiterate** compositions at two hundred dollars apiece.

In return for the most **unmitigated trash** ... he filled his empty pockets with dollars coined out of **Republican fanaticism.**

Impartiality, like news itself, is whatever the publisher says it is.

Cartoon in Vanity Fair, December 29, 1860

BADGERING HIM.
J. G. B. — Bow! Wow! Come Out, Mr. Lincoln!

In 1896, Adolph Ochs buys the New York Times. Many cite his statement of intent as one of the earliest, **best** expressions of journalism's highest ideals...

It will be my earnest aim that the New York Times give the news ... **impartially, without fear or favor, regardless of party, sect, or interest** involved ... to invite intelligent discussion from all shades of opinion...

People usually end the quote at this point, but **he** goes on...

... Nor will there be a departure from the general tone ... unless it be ... to intensify its devotion to the cause of **sound money** and **tariff reform**...

... and in its advocacy of the **lowest tax** consistent with good government and **no more government** than is absolutely necessary to protect society...

After **impartially** reviewing the facts, he sees *little* role for government in *local* affairs.

Yet *all* around him, there's grinding, dehumanizing poverty. It's right there in the eyes of the boys who *sell* his paper.

Perhaps after an equally "impartial" review, Och's great-grandson and current Times publisher might have reached a different conclusion.

Still, the Times positions itself as the paper that favors information over narrative; the "facts" over the readers' assumptions, emotions, and values.

It's journalism's first giant step toward an unreachable goal -- because it's unprofitable to ignore your readers' emotions, assumptions, and values.

And it's impossible to ignore your own.

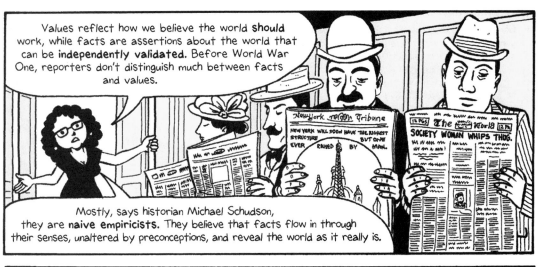

Values reflect how we believe the world **should** work, while facts are assertions about the world that can be **independently validated.** Before World War One, reporters don't distinguish much between facts and values.

Mostly, says historian Michael Schudson, they are **naive empiricists.** They believe that facts flow in through their senses, unaltered by preconceptions, and reveal the world as it really is.

Those facts fit neatly into a vision of a world that is **cruel,** but also rich with **opportunity.**

This is a generation raised on Horatio Alger's dime novels, in which the humblest of orphans could ascend into the middle class -- if they worked **hard.**

But in the 1920s, a deep cynicism sets in, as damaged men returned home, many with personal photos of comrades dying in the trenches they had dug -- hideous and meaningless deaths of millions of young men.

In Europe and America, there's growing awareness that governments lie, that newspapers lie, that long-held values do not fit the new facts and that it may be impossible to really **know** anything.

99

Some of the disillusioned turn to novels of gritty realism...

I had seen nothing sacred, and the things that were glorious had no glory and the sacrifices were like the stockyards at Chicago if nothing was done with the meat except to bury it.

For us lads of eighteen ... the idea of authority ... was associated in our minds with a greater insight and a more humane wisdom.

But ... the first bombardment showed us our mistake ... and under it the world as they had taught it to us broke in pieces.

Some turn to poetry...

If you could hear, at every jolt, the blood
Come gargling from the froth-corrupted lungs,
Obscene as cancer, bitter as the cud
Of vile, incurable sores on innocent tongues --
My friend, you would not tell with such high zest
To children ardent for some desperate glory,
The old Lie; Dulce et decorum est Pro patria mori.

A new European art movement revels in meaninglessness...

After Duchamp.

What good did the theories of the philosophers do us? ... We are. We argue, we dispute, we get excited. The rest is sauce.

The beginnings of Dada were not the beginnings of an art, but of a **disgust**. Disgust with the magnificence of philosophers who for 3000 years have been explaining everything to us...

Like everything in life, Dada is useless. Dada is without pretension, as life should be.

Meanwhile, the wartime propaganda industry trolls for peacetime markets. Edward Bernays, Sigmund Freud's nephew, is a public relations pioneer.

In almost every act of our daily lives ... we are dominated by the ... small number of persons ... who pull the wires which control the public mind.

Among his triumphs: promoting smoking as a symbol of women's liberation --

-- though he vehemently opposed his wife's smoking -- for health reasons.

Some papers seek to distinguish themselves from unabashed manipulators like Bernays by making even more of their own objectivity.

But after World War One, one of journalism's greatest theorists, Walter Lippmann, accuses the elite press of **strangling objectivity** in its crib.

Judged simply by their **product**, men like **Mr. Ochs** ... believe that ... **civilization** [will] decay unless their idea of what is patriotic is permitted to temper the curiosity of their readers.

They believe that **edification** is more important than **veracity**. They believe it profoundly, violently ... They **preen** themselves upon it.

Advocates ... argue that true opinion will prevail over error.

True opinions can prevail only if the **facts** ... are **known**; if they are not known, **false** ideas are just as effective ... if not a little **more** effective.

There can be no higher law in journalism than to tell the truth and shame the devil.

LIPPMANN DOES NOT EXPECT journalists to be entirely objective, but he urges them to renounce creeds and use the *methods of science* to discipline their minds and scrutinize their facts. He sees journalistic objectivity more as a process than a state of mind.

Some media critics view it more reductively, as a writing style: simple sentences presenting the facts in order of importance, no emotion, no first-person pronouns.

And although "interpretive journalism" thrives after the war, political columns are clearly marked and more stories are bylined, so readers know *what* and *who* they are reading.

Soon, the "yellow" that had dominated much of mainstream journalism gives way to mottled gray. Neutral colors better suit the evolving news business.

Back when papers were numerous and noisy, says historian Daniel Hallin, they wrapped themselves in the First Amendment's protection of a vigorous marketplace of ideas.

But as the news business *consolidates*—killing off or absorbing the little papers—the big ones grow increasingly influential, setting off alarms for the rich and powerful. The news barons hear those alarms. They're rich and powerful, too.

No longer are newspapers scrappy kids grabbing for snatches of readership.

They need to be legitimized, to show themselves *worthy* of their power by adhering to a moral philosophy that reveres *facts* above all, facts not naively interpreted, but *validated*.

Objectivity works to repel the attacks of critics, like a kind of ethical pepper spray.

All this sets the stage for the era that inspires so much nostalgia in some media circles; the mid- to late twentieth century, when the values of *today's* titans of journalism were formed, the era of the great newspapers and objective TV newscasts.

It's a time when another new technology comes along and changes everything, again.

The GOLDEN AGE of OBJECTIVITY

The American media business is a creature of politics and technology.

At America's founding, subsidized postage for newspapers fosters a rancorous press that politicians tolerate in order to forge a sense of national identity.

Later, the telegraph and steam-driven rotary presses serve an exploding population of immigrants and workers at the very moment a fractured political culture is engaged in a furious debate over what America stands for.

But in the mid-twentieth century, national *consensus* is Washington's top priority. And for the first time in American history, it's the media's top priority, too.

The infant TV networks depend on ad revenue to fund production, so they need audiences of unprecedented size.

Also, networks rely on the government for broadcast licenses and most of the news. *Also*, they have to comply with a new regulation (enacted in1949) requiring them to *set aside* time to present *all* sides of the controversial issues they cover.

Suddenly, *controversy* is *bad* for the TV biz, and that's good for the government.

The result is *symbiosis*. To wage the Cold War, the government needs political consensus and ideological conformity. To be profitable, TV needs to appeal to the American mainstream. Both thrive by narrowing debate and bottling up cultural and political outliers.

By the mid-1950s, more than half the nation's living rooms have a TV set, which serves as a kind of national mirror. It reflects a populace that is white, Christian, and middle-class. It has no

accent. It defines normal. It defines America.

When Walter Cronkite ends his CBS newscast with his rock-solid assertion, it's a sweet finish to his nightly suppertime slice of reality: facts, unseasoned and served deadpan. (His verdict on Vietnam is an exception reflecting a changing consensus.)

Cronkite's steady voice assures us that despite rising anxiety over nuclear holocaust, everything is under control. One poll anoints him the most trusted man in America.

We call him Uncle Walter.

The Communist menace is real. So is the threat of nuclear war. TV news starts with that premise. But while the newscasts project cool, the public affairs shows turn up the heat.

Communism is a **creeping, sinuous** ideology that **destroys man's soul**...

...The contents of this NBC News program represent no editorial opinion...

Historian Nancy Bernhard notes that most reporters of the era see no conflict between objectivity and anti-Communism. It's the only possible position.

In 1951, a government film advises kids to **duck and cover** when they see the nuclear flash. It plays in schools and on television.

Some TV listings call it a documentary.

In 1953, the government builds "Doom Town" in Yucca Flats, Nevada, fills it with mannequins, and drops a bomb on it. It's on every network.

AN ATTACK IS NOT TAKING PLACE

In 1957, CBS broadcasts "A Day Called X," the mass evacuation of Portland, Oregon, in response to a hypothetical nuclear attack. Portland Mayor Terry Shrunk takes part.

... In less than three hours an H-bomb might fall over Portland.

None of this seems weird at the time.

Historian Daniel Hallin divides the journalists' world into three spheres...

The donut **hole** is the sphere of **consensus**, "the region of motherhood and apple pie." Unquestionable values and unchallengeable truths.

The donut is journalism's sweet spot: the sphere of **legitimate controversy**. Here issues are undecided, debated, probed.

Election coverage is on the donut, as are discussions of social, economic, even war policies, once they are nudged **out** of the sphere of consensus by people in **authority**. That's where "objective" journalism thrives.

The sphere of **deviance** is the air around the donut. Limbo.

The place for people and opinions that the "mainstream of the society reject as unworthy of being heard."

Objective reporters don't go there.

In fact, says Hallin, the press plays gatekeeper, by defining and **defending** "the limits of acceptable political conduct."

But it's much easier to see the **whole** donut from a distance. A hundred years should be enough.

In 1909, Missouri Senator W. J. Stone strikes a waiter in a Pullman dining car, but is acquitted of assault: bad service is deemed sufficient "provocation." The Times condemns the decision and rebukes Senator Stone...

"The Senator insisted on the use of the term 'to slap.' 'I did not strike a man,' he explained, 'I slapped a nigger.' Everyone who travels much, and uses the dining cars, can sympathize with the Senator. The service is frequently bad."

"But he ought not to have slapped him ... No provocation justifies loss of self-control in a United States Senator..."

"Doubtless his contempt for the Negro is an inheritance, as he is a Kentuckian by birth... But his argument that 'slapping a nigger' is not 'striking a man' will not hold good in many States of the Union."

Let's stipulate that in the twenty-first century, hitting a waiter who is late with your lunch is inexcusable, **actionable** behavior -- a view that fits squarely in the donut hole of consensus.

In 1909, it falls into the sphere of legitimate controversy. So the Times "objectively" examines the case and concludes that, all things considered, the racist Senator has dishonored himself and his office.

What falls into the sphere of **deviance**? The **waiter's** perspective. It's irrelevant.

In fact, even to **consider** his side of the story, or the grievances of Pullman waiters generally, would smack of unseemly **advocacy**. The **legitimate** debate extends only to the damage done to the dignity of the Senate.

So, the sphere of consensus **moves**. To stay in step, the national media have to track it in the moment. Not easy.

These days, main-stream journalists tend to be wealthier, more educated, more coastal, and less religious that most Americans. There's no guaranteed affinity.

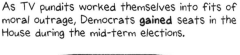

They could try to **guess** what folks think out there in "flyover country." Or they could check their **own** pulses and extrapolate.

Both methods failed miserably during the 1998 Bill Clinton - Monica Lewinsky scandal. Clinton's approval ratings rose swiftly and stayed high. The public was more disgusted by the obsessive coverage than the President's lies.

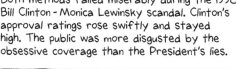

As TV pundits worked themselves into fits of moral outrage, Democrats **gained** seats in the House during the mid-term elections.

GEORGE WILL   COKIE ROBERTS   ⓐⓑⓒ

Polls would seem to be the **scientific** way to chart consensus, but of course, wording changes everything. Example: A January 2003 Pew poll...

When people were asked whether they would "favor or oppose taking military action in Iraq to end Saddam Hussein's rule," **68%** favored it.

But when pollsters added this clause "... even if it meant that U.S. forces might suffer thousands of casualties," only **43%** favored it.

So how does a reporter best serve the news consumer? Not by guessing at the consensus, or taking one's own pulse. Not by following polls.

Not by mechanically allotting equal space to two sides (rarely more than two) without context, even when one side is lying or misinformed.

Or by selecting the facts to fit a viewpoint or promote an outcome.

Probably, it's best for reporters to **start** by figuring out how **they** really feel about the issues they cover. Or, as **some** suggest...

...how **not** to feel. Former Washington Post executive editor Len Downie says that when he got that job, he stopped **voting**.

I had the last word as to whether or not the paper was being fair in its reporting ... and I didn't want to take a position, even in my own mind, on them.

So, despite all the information -- all you **know** about the political environment of Washington, DC -- you are able to **not** make up your **mind**?

Yes, actually it comes fairly easily to me ... to see all sides of most issues.

Does he also say he can **bend forks** with his mind? You know, some people can do remarkable things.

Political writer Michael Kinsley has been the editor of the New Republic, Harper's magazine, and Slate.

This notion that journalists ought to be sort of political, ideological eunuchs ... is just hopeless.

The question isn't whether they hold opinions, but whether they suppress those opinions -- to the extent they can -- when they do their work.

But some reporters argue that if you stake out a position, you get **invested**, like the guy who buys a car and then tries to convince **you** to buy the same model.

And if you happen to report from one of the most **polarized** places on the planet, being a political **eunuch** starts to look pretty good.

Ethan Bronner reports from Israel for the New York Times.

I have views on what should happen, or what has happened, but I think the most important view I have is to keep my mind open to the idea that my own view may be **wrong**.

Mediterranean Sea

WEST BANK

Jerusalem

GAZA

ISRAEL   JORDAN

EGYPT

If you force yourself **not** to come to a conclusion about a difficult issue, to leave yourself open, you will **stay** more open.

THERE ARE TWO ISSUES HERE. One is the challenge reporters face in confronting a raft of data, confirming it, distilling it, writing it, and yet forming no opinions about it.

The other is what to do with those opinions, however fluid, once they form.

There are rules about such things.

Most reporters may not participate in or contribute to campaigns. In some places, they may not register for a political party. They may display no signs, march in no rallies, and according to some media ethicists, they should not write their elected representatives, or volunteer in their church's public relations office.

They can vote. (It's a secret ballot after all.) Then they should just shut up.

News organizations figure that if reporters act on their conviction, editors would have to bar them from covering certain stories, because the public wouldn't trust them to be fair, even if they were. It's about appearances.

As we have seen, hypersensitivity to the appearance of objectivity can lead to some lousy reporting. A reporter should be able to call a lie a lie.

But in American newspapers, official statements come first. Challenges appear way down, sometimes after you turn the page. News analysis comes in a box. Newscasts rarely go past the official statements.

U.S. newspapers try to build a wall between the editorial pages and the news pages. They have different editors. In the twentieth century, it was a fundamental principle of journalism. Not so much in the twenty-first century.

Now entire cable news channels report the world through obvious political prisms.

Now websites that serve as primary news sources for many Americans make no secret of their ideological leanings.

The reason is the same as always. New technology gives rise to new business models. The model now emerging is based on tracking online behavior and targeting ads to individuals. Also *slowly* emerging: an increasing willingness to *pay* for some information and cultural products online.

Once again, new technology reflects and reinforces the political culture—now *splintered*. The result: food fight!

DISCLOSURE

Thirty years ago, we didn't have so many options...

ABC, NBC, or CBS?

But now it seems we have to make crucial decisions all the time.

Whole life or term?

IRA? Roth IRA? 401K? Hi-cap, low-cap, decaf...?

HMO, PPO, or POS?

Mastectomy or lumpectomy?

You can't negotiate the modern world without absorbing a ton of data. With so much to digest, do you really need to know how reporters **feel**?

Or is that too much information?

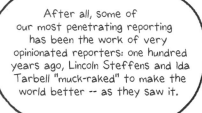
After all, some of our most penetrating reporting has been the work of very opinionated reporters: one hundred years ago, Lincoln Steffens and Ida Tarbell "muck-raked" to make the world better -- as they saw it.

There is no man more dangerous, in a position of power, than he who refuses to accept ... that **all** a man does should make for rightness and soundness, that even the fixing of a tariff rate **must be moral.**

THE HISTORY OF THE STANDARD OIL COMPANY
BY IDA M. TARBELL

McCLURE'S MAGAZINE
NOVEMBER, 1903
The Labor Boss
The Trust's New Tool
By
RAY STANNARD BAKER
New York
By
LINCOLN STEFFENS

Today, reporters aren't supposed to make the world better. Their job is to tell you what's going on, so **you** can make it better.

...

So, would you trust them more if you knew more about them?

New media types say that in the age of <u>links,</u> journalists can hold the trust of their audience **only** if they **disclose** -- online -- their views, values, process and, whenever possible, their sources.

Transparency is the new <u>objectivity.</u>

Author David Weinberger chronicles and forecasts the impact of the Web.

Transparency gives the reader information by which she can **undo** some of the unintended effects of the ever-present biases. Transparency brings us to reliability the way objectivity used to.

Objectivity without transparency increasingly will look like arrogance.... Why should we trust what one person -- with the best of intentions -- insists is true when we instead could have a web of evidence, ideas, and argument?

Objectivity is a trust mechanism you rely on when your medium can't do links. Now our medium **can.**

Bloggers almost always opt for full disclosure.

Jeff Jarvis, former newspaper editor, columnist, and founder of Entertainment Weekly, left old media and launched the blog Buzzmachine. His bio exhaustively covers his business and media ties, stocks, voting record, religion, views on energy policy, school prayer, Howard Stern...

...I am a post-9/11 hawk.... I am pro-choice.... I believe government must find some way to fix America's health care.... I do not think big media are too big because there is new competition.... I support Israel's right to exist...

Time magazine's James Poniewozik says political reporters should disclose their votes, and then disprove charges of **bias** by doing great journalism.

More damaging, in the age of authenticity, is **phoniness** -- in this case, acting as if we were dispassionate **marble gods**.

It's time to leave that Potemkin Olympus and **admit** that, like responsible citizens, we care about elections. And then **prove** that, like responsible professionals, we care about the **truth** more.

Journalists love to argue about the pros and cons of disclosure, but sometimes disclosing is conflated with the idea of forsaking "objectivity."

These are separate issues.

Reporters who reveal themselves still have a duty to report responsibly. In fact, some say it increases their incentive to be scrupulously fair.

That is, unless they react to the scrutiny by suspending all judgment, or overcompensating with fake balance that distorts coverage.

Not a problem for most talk show hosts, columnists, or bloggers. Most are explicitly opinionated. They succeed by serving the needs, interests, and **biases** of the communities they help create.

NIGHT

The World

BRYAN SPEAKS ON ALL GREAT ISSUES.

Just like the old days.

But news reporters are expected to deliver reliable information. If they reveal themselves to earn audience trust, **they** have to trust the audience not to **pre**-judge their work. Which is impossible.

News consumers **say** they want objectivity, but they **choose** news outlets that reflect their views. Personal information about reporters is irrelevant, until they run afoul of those views. Then it becomes ammunition.

In 2006, Stanford University's Shanto Iyengar and Washington Post poll director Richard Morin designed a study to test that very proposition.

They showed Democrats, Republicans, and independents **identical** news stories with different labels -- like Fox News, CNN, and NPR -- and asked them to choose which to read. The stories ranged from politics to sports to travel.

Independents had no strong preference. Republicans overwhelmingly preferred Fox, and soundly rejected CNN and NPR. Democrats soundly rejected Fox -- but showed only "lukewarm" preferences for CNN and NPR.

Perhaps Democrats' brand loyalty is weaker because they find CNN and NPR content **insufficiently slanted.**

Or Democrats are **less** inclined to seek out news coverage that **confirms** their view of the world.

Other studies show similar differences between Republicans and Democrats. I could review some of those findings -- but **BOY** would I look biased!

Not that it would matter. I have a show on public radio. The research suggests that news consumers already have made up their minds about me.

So I think reporters should disclose their potential conflicts of interest, sources, and methods whenever they can. That's relevant context. The rest is just... static.

...scoliosis when I was 12... but it went away...

·THE FOOL·

·THE WORLD·

·QUEEN of PENTACLES·

·THE MATRIX·

116

THE MATRIX IN ME

You can see it when you look out your window ... when you turn on your television ... when you go to work.

It is the world that has been pulled over your eyes to **blind** you from the **truth**.

What truth?

That ... like everyone else ... you were ... born into a prison that you cannot smell or taste or touch. A prison for your mind.

More precisely, the prison OF your mind. We **think** we know when we are being impulsive and when we are rational. But new research shows that our actions and beliefs are driven more by impulses and biases we never knew we had.

Let's start with **impulses.** When we get butterflies in the stomach, we assume our brain has sent a message **down** to our **gut.** But more likely, our gut has sent a message **up** to our **brain.**

Our gut has a separate, autonomous nervous system. It produces its own seratonin and dopamine. It makes its own decisions about the world.

For instance, warmth makes the gut feel mmm, mmm good.

In a 2008 study, researchers, pretending to be fumbling with stuff, momentarily handed their cups of either **hot** or **iced** coffee to people, and then asked them to rate an unknown person's personality based on a packet of information.

The test subjects who held the **hot** cup rated that person noticeably higher for "**warmth**" than those holding the iced coffee.

In another study, test subjects who held a **hot** therapeutic pad were more likely to choose a gift for a **friend.** When they held a **cold** pad, they chose something for **themselves.**

How **rational** is that?

On the other hand... ahhh...

Research suggests that often conscious choice is an **illusion** -- leading some people to ponder whether there really is such a thing as **free will.**

In 2008, neuroscientists at the Max Planck Institute in Leipzig conducted a study to see what happens in our brains just before we make a decision.

You decide which button to press and when to press it. Just remember **when** you made up your mind.

This is potentially a big deal. Because if we don't know that we've already decided -- how can we apply our **reason** to the choices we make? Can we circumvent our unconscious?

Watching live brain scans, researchers predict people's decisions up to **seven seconds before the test subjects were even aware of making them.**

Most of our **biases** are unconscious too. I'm giving expert Shankar Vedantam (from whom I took the "Matrix" analogy) this page to illustrate a couple.

Shankar Vedantam
THE HIDDEN BRAIN

Overweight job applicants are widely perceived to be less intelligent, lazier, and more immoral than identically qualified applicants of normal weight.

In one study, job applicants who merely **sat down next to an overweight person** were ranked lower.

"HIRED!"

Next, gender bias. A university study divided volunteers into two groups...

Subordinates have often described **James** as someone who is tough, yet outgoing and personable. He is known to reward individual contributions and has worked hard to maximize employees' creativity.

...and gave them the exact same information, except for **one detail**.

Subordinates have often described **Andrea** as someone who is tough, yet outgoing and personable. She is known to reward individual contributions and has worked hard to maximize employees' creativity.

Asked to guesstimate how likeable Andrea and James were: **75%** of the volunteers thought James was more likeable than Andrea; **80%** preferred to have James be their boss.

James is a born leader!

...so fair!

Andrea sounds pushy.

...and manipulative.

It's probably not shocking to learn that even the most enlightened of us probably are a **little bit** racist.

For more than a decade, researchers have tested **millions** of people for unconscious biases with the **Implicit Association Test.** Here's how it works...

Project Implicit

Faces flash on a screen: depending on the bias being tested, they could be black and white; old and young; male and female; fat and thin; and so on.

Without pausing, you're asked to click the right key to identify, say, the black face, and then the left key to identify the white face. Easy.

Then you do the same with positive and negative **words.**

Then black and white faces appear **with** the weighted words randomly right and left, and you have to click to indicate the positive and negative words without pausing or thinking...

They found that more than 80% of whites respond more positively to white faces...

...and so do 50% of blacks.

Does this mean we're prejudiced? Yes -- if we **consciously** agree with what our unconscious minds reveal. But if we are aware of our biases, we can deal with them.

Anyone can take the test online. Worth it: **implicit.harvard.edu.**

You would assume that concrete evidence would dislodge false facts. Not so. If a statement is repeated often enough, people will believe it, **even if it labeled as false.**

An example: In 2005, a federal agency issued a flyer to combat myths about a flu vaccine, labeling common assertions as true or false.

FALSE: The side effects are worse than the flu. **TRUE:** The flu vaccine saves lives.

One study found that within 30 minutes, older people misremembered 28% of the false statements as true. It took younger people three days to misremember.

~~TRUE~~ ~~FALSE~~: The side effects are worse than the flu.

In both cases, the "true-false" flyer **lowered** their intention to get vaccinated.

And if we're **predisposed** to believe the myths, we'll actively avoid hearing contradictory information.

In 1967, psychologists had college students listen to various tape-recorded messages about smoking that were obscured by static. At any point the students could press a button to **temporarily reduce** the static.

The smokers often pressed to remove static from a message **disputing** the **link** between smoking and cancer, but were less likely than nonsmokers to "de-static" messages **affirming** a smoking-cancer link.

The Surgeon General reports...

Not sure what brand they smoked, but they definitely liked their facts filtered.

Researcher John Bullock exposed volunteers to an ad by an abortion-rights group charging Supreme Court nominee John Roberts with supporting a violent anti-abortion group. Then Bullock told them that the ad was **misleading** and had been withdrawn.

When a bomb ripped through my clinic, I almost lost my life.

CHOOSE JUSTICE

OPPOSE JOHN ROBERTS
Call Your Senator: 202-224-3121

56% of Democrats disapproved of Roberts **before** they saw the ad. After they saw it, **80%** disapproved. **After** they heard it had been withdrawn, **72%** still had a bad opinion.

But **opinions** are one thing. Facts do change minds, right?

Researchers Brendan Nyhan and Jason Reifler showed a group of Republican volunteers solid evidence that there were no weapons of mass destruction in Iraq before the 2003 U.S. invasion.

Iraq Survey Group Final Report

+

Report of the U.N. Monitoring, Verification and Inspection Commission

= No WMDs

Prior to hearing the proof, roughly a **third** believed Iraq had hidden or discarded those weapons before the U.S. invasion. But after they heard the evidence, nearly **two-thirds** of them believed it!

Brendan Nyhan -- **how is this possible?**

People were so successful at bringing to mind reasons the correction was **wrong** that they actually ended up being **more convinced** than the people who **didn't** receive the correction.

Do I **contradict** myself? Very well, then I contradict myself. I am large, I contain multitudes.

Walt Whitman was ... atypical. Most of us are distressed by contradictory information, especially information that contradicts our beliefs. The deeper our belief, the deeper our **distress.**

Psychologist Leon Festinger called it **cognitive dissonance.**

Suppose an individual believes something with his whole heart; suppose further ... that he has taken irrevocable actions because of it.

"Finally, suppose that he is presented with evidence, unequivocal and undeniable evidence, that his belief is **wrong.** What will happen?"

"The individual will frequently emerge, not only unshaken, but even **more** convinced of the truth of his beliefs than ever before."

"Indeed, he may even show a new fervor for ... converting other people to his view."

Festinger derived his theory from observing a cult that predicted a great flood would engulf the Earth in December 1954.

The leader, Dorothy Martin, received the message from Sananda (Jesus) and the "Guardians" from the planet Clarion, via "automatic writing."

On December 21, at midnight, the Guardians will **rescue** us! We must dispose of our property and cut our ties with the world!

Until midnight there was joyful anticipation...

...but after midnight, only despair and desperation...

...until dawn brought new tidings of triumph and hope.

Sananda just sent me a message -- that your devotion has **saved** the whole world!

Next, Martin claimed the **Rapture** would occur at 6 p.m. on December 24.

The Guardians were here! But they didn't want to start a **riot**...

...so they made themselves **invisible** to non-believers!

The believers were trapped. They could explain away the facts -- but to be secure in their faith they had to convince **others**.

This scenario plays out all the time with all kinds of believers.

Skeptics say, "I'll **believe** it when I **see** it."

Maybe they shouldn't.

A cautionary tale from Alan Baddeley's "Your Memory: A User's Guide":

Australian eyewitness expert Donald Thomson once appeared on live TV to discuss the **unreliability** of eyewitness testimony.

Some time later, he was arrested -- identified by a woman as the man who had raped her.

Donald Thomson   LIVE

But I was on **live** TV when the rape occurred -- an assistant police commissioner was on the same show!

And I suppose you've got **Jesus Christ** and the **Queen of England**, too.

Eventually, the investigators realized that the rape victim had been watching the program when she was attacked.

She had conflated Thomson's face with the rapist's, proving Thomson's point about eyewitness testimony.

POLICE

He must have been thrilled.

As for photos and documents -- it's **always** easy to doubt the truth of those...

It's a fake!

History is awash with dubious photos. But now **anyone** can fake a photo. And everyone does. It's what Farhad Manjoo, author of the book "True Enough," calls the **photoshopification** of society.

LOCH NESS MONSTER

SASQUATCH

PALIN POOLSIDE PACKING RIFLE

The big threat of photoshopification is **not** that we will **believe** documents and photos that are fake.

It's that we'll find it easier to **dis-believe** documents and photos that are **real**. When it's convenient.

SOAP

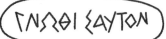

BACK BEFORE THERE WERE MEDIA OUTLETS, an ancient
traveler noted a fateful warning carved on the temple of the Oracle of
Delphi (a notorious newsmaker). It read: "Know thyself."

Now the media cover the world like cloudy water. We have to
consciously filter it. In an era when everything is asserted and anything
denied, we really need to know who we are and how our brains work.

Humans run on emotion, assumption, and impulse. We can't function
on logic alone. People who can't feel pleasure or preference because of damage to the orbital
prefrontal cortex are paralyzed by the simple decisions most of us make effortlessly every day.
The blue pen or the black pen? Mary or Sue? Any choice—whether of a mate or a breakfast
cereal—engulfs them in a quicksand of pros and cons.

But emotion, assumption, and impulse also allow us to weave cozy cocoons of
unexamined prejudice and received wisdom. They shield us from the pain of unwelcome
information. William James once said that "the greatest enemy of any one of our truths may
be the rest of our truths." So you have to ask yourself . . . well, here's how James Fitzjames
Stephen framed the key questions back in 1873 . . .

**What do you think of yourself?
What do you think of the world?...** They
are riddles of the Sphinx, and in some way or other
we must deal with them. If we decide to leave them
unanswered, that is a choice; if we waver in our
answer, that, too, is a choice: but whatever choice
we make, we make it at our peril...

We stand on a mountain pass in
the midst of whirling snow and blinding mist
through which we get glimpses now and then of paths
which may be deceptive. If we stand still we shall be
frozen to death. If we take the wrong road we shall
be dashed to pieces. We do not certainly know
whether there is any right one.
What must we do?

THE INFLUENCING MACHINES

So as we stand on the mountain -- which way do we go?

Instinctively we drift toward people like ourselves, flocking together like birds of a feather. This is called **homophily**. It shapes our worldview.

The mirror built by homophily reflects and reaffirms our perspective.

BROOKE'S WORLDVIEW

WOODSTOCK

This is unhealthy. It can lead to an array of digitally borne diseases.

Many say that the Internet's ability to link like-minded souls everywhere fosters the creation of virtually impermeable echo chambers.

The echo chambers give rise to cybercascades: when a "fact" sent by one person spreads in a geometric progression to others until millions of people around the world potentially believe it.

GLOBAL WARMING IS BALONEY
DRIVE THRU OPEN 24 HOURS

Cut off from dissenters, the chambers fill with an unjustified sense of certainty. It's called **incestuous amplification**, a term first applied to isolated military planners who base their strategies on flawed assumptions.

Incestuous amplification can occur in any sphere, even without the Internet. But it helps.

Real estate bubble? **Fuggedabboutit!**

Hint: When you hear a group of guys called "Masters of the Universe," **run!**

Cass Sunstein cites many studies showing how people who talk only to like-minded others grow more extreme. They **marginalize the moderates**...

...and **demonize** dissenters. The greatest danger of echo chambers is unjustified **extremism**. It's an ongoing **threat** to our **democracy**.

Author Nicholas Carr has a different fear: "Is Google making us stupid?"

Media are not just passive **channels** of information. They supply the **stuff** of thought, but they also shape the **process** of thought.

Over the past few years I've had an uncomfortable sense that someone, or something, has been tinkering with my brain, remapping the neural circuitry, reprogramming the memory.

Immersing myself in a book or a lengthy article used to be easy ... Now my concentration often starts to drift after two or three pages.

...Once I was a scuba diver in the sea of words. Now I zip along the surface like a guy on a Jet-Ski.

Technology does change our brains. Humanity's first use of handheld tools coincided with the growth of the prefrontal cortex, as well as grammatical language and more complex social networks.

So it's likely that our brains **will** process information differently in our increasingly interconnected environment. We'll also have the ability to rush ahead of evolution -- by **implanting** new technology.

Does that creep you out?

Actually, I'm **not** creeped out, and not because I'm especially optimistic about human nature. I just take my cues from history. And the history of communications is full of... histrionics.

People always see the future and despair that the latest gizmo will destroy our concentration, memory, communities, our mental and physical **health**...

Consider television. On May 9, 1961, Federal Communications Commission chairman Newton N. Minow said **this** to a convention of the National Association of Broadcasters...

I invite each of you to sit down in front of your television set when your station goes on the air and stay there ... until the station signs off.

I can assure you that what you will observe is a vast wasteland.

Actually, the TV scares do have some very good data behind them.

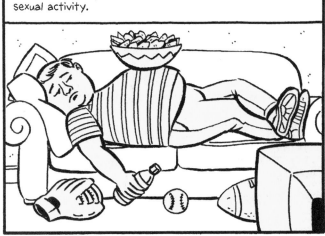

Study after study has found strong links between excessive TV exposure and childhood obesity, smoking, and sexual activity.

But radio also was condemned. A 1936 issue of Gramophone cited research asserting that "children often *lie* awake in bed restless and fearful, or wake up screaming, as a result of nightmares brought on by mystery stories."

WELCOME, MY FRIENDS, TO THE INNER SANCTUM...!

Now we celebrate radio's golden age because "we had to use our imaginations."

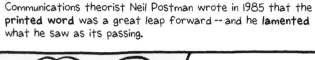

Communications theorist Neil Postman wrote in 1985 that the **printed word** was a great leap forward -- and he **lamented** what he saw as its passing.

Most of our modern ideas about the uses of the intellect were formed by the printed word, as were our ideas about education, knowledge, truth, and information...

"...as typography moves to the periphery of our culture ... the seriousness, clarity and, above all, value of public discourse dangerously declines."

But a century earlier, assiduous reading was itself suspect. Especially for girls.

"Foolish parents ... exhaust their children's brains ... with complex and multiple studies... The evils are becoming noticed in all quarters. Some of the prize girls soon find their way to **insane asylums**..."

THE SANITARIAN,

As Gutenberg's press took off, so did fears of information overload. In 1545, Conrad Gesner assembled a "Universal Library," while complaining of the...

...confusing and harmful abundance of books...

He decided to list only books written in Greek, Latin, and Hebrew.

Barnaby Rich, an English soldier, wrote in 1613 that books...

...so **overcharge** the world that it is not able to digest the abundance of **idle matter** that is every day hatched and brought forth into the world!

Rich himself authored some 26 books, including works on the military, manners, morals, and several romances.

In 1985, Tibor Braun coins the term "Barnaby Rich syndrome" -- the conviction that "it is always the other author who writes and publishes too much."

Ye Olde Bookshoppe

In Plato's "Phaedrus," Socrates derides the invention of writing, with a story in which the Egyptian god who invented the alphabet brags to a king.

This will make the Egyptians **wiser** and give them better **memories.**

The inventor is not always the best judge of his own inventions. This discovery of yours will create **forgetfulness** in the learners' souls -- they will trust to the external written characters and **not remember** of themselves.

Which bring us 'round to the wisdom offered up by author Douglas Adams.

Anything that is in the world when you're born is normal and ordinary and is just a natural part of the way the world works.

Anything that's invented between when you're 15 and 35 is new and exciting and revolutionary.

Anything invented after you're 35 is against the natural order of things.

Adams offered the best advice for these terrifying times when, in 1979, he described his (then) imaginary "Hitchhiker's Guide to the Galaxy."

[It] had about 100 tiny flat press buttons and a screen about four inches square on which any one of a million "pages" could be summoned at a moment's notice.

It looked insanely complicated, and this was one of the reasons why ... it ... had the words "DON'T PANIC" printed on it in large friendly letters.

DON'T PANIC

... UM, PANIC?*

But why shouldn't I panic?

There's plenty of research to back it up!

The belief that too much choice breeds apathy and paralysis draws strength from a 1999 study by Sheena Iyengar and Mark Lepper. They set up a tasting booth in a fancy supermarket and offered one group **six** varieties of jam.

Don't forget your discount coupon!

Later, 30% of this group used their discount coupon to buy jam.

Then they offered a second group **24** varieties.

Don't forget your discount coupon!

Of this group, only 3% used their discount coupons -- an astounding difference. All those choices seemed to **kill the motivation to choose anything.**

Ten years later, Swiss psychologist Benjamin Scheibehenne and colleagues tried to replicate the jam study but failed to get the same results. So they conducted a meta-analysis of **50** studies on the impact of choice.

We found no empirical evidence for choice overload.

Wallpaper

Mutual Funds

Perfumes

Dating Partners

Chee...

Jelly Beans

So why is **information** overload seen as one of the pervasive maladies of modern life? Media theorist Clay Shirky says many people confuse information overload with **filter failure.**

If you took the contents of an average Barnes and Noble, dumped it into the streets, and said to someone, "There's some works of Auden in there, there's some Plato in there. Wade on in and you'll find what you like."

If you waded in -- you know what you would get?

All this junk.

The reason we don't experience information overload problem in a bookstore or a library is that we're used to the cataloging system.

So, the real question is, how do we design filters for the Web that let us find our way through this particular abundance of information?

The fact is, those filters already are out there... a constellation of aggregators, social networks, traditional news outlets, and more and more...

You don't have to go it alone. You have friends out there.

But **do** we have friends out there? Or are we **losing touch** with the people who really matter by replacing them with loose ties to people we don't know?

YES! In 1985, most Americans had three people with whom they discussed "important matters." In 2004, they had just two. And the number of people who confided in **no one** had nearly tripled.

They may have 600 friends on Facebook and e-mail 25 people a day, but they are **not** discussing matters that are personally important.

NO! People use the Internet to **increase** the number of people that they interact with in the world ... and they don't use those devices as substitutes for other kinds of human contact...

There are lonely people ... and the availability of these technologies does help them stay isolated. But for the vast majority of people that we look at in our research, they say these technologies are **adding** to their social well-being.

Duke sociologist Lynn Smith-Lovin

Pew researcher Lee Rainie

OK, Lee Rainie, but what about the echo chambers? Don't we create little worlds online where we never have to confront people who are different from us?

On the contrary! We found that Internet users and cell phone users had bigger and more diverse networks. For instance, frequent Internet users and bloggers are much more likely to confide in someone who is of another race...

...and those who share photos online are more likely to discuss important matters with someone who is a member of another political party.

In fact, those who are the most technologically adept actually are **not** in the echo chamber pattern; they are actually **seeking out** and finding out more arguments opposed to their views...

They behave like information **omnivores**, scanning every horizon they can. They can't help but bump into stuff that doesn't agree with them.

Md 2

It turns out that using a device to reach out and touch someone -- like, say, your mother -- is not necessarily a poor substitute for face-to-face contact.

Researchers asked young girls to do a stressful task. Afterward, some girls spoke to their mothers in person; other girls called them on the phone. Both groups of girls experienced the **same** drop in the stress hormone cortisol (though the phone call took longer).

So, cell phone addiction may be our way of medicating **against isolation**. And information addiction may inoculate us **against echo chambers**.

Maybe the same technology that gives rise to digital diseases actually holds the CURE.

But what about the research that finds our ability to **think** is being diminished by all the time we spend in perpetual motion online?

Nick Carr says we need time for efficient data collection **and** time for inefficient contemplation. But we don't have that much time. And it's changing us.

There's a saying among neuroscientists that "neurons that fire together, wire together." When you practice a certain skill, the circuits get stronger, and the area of your brain dedicated to performing the skill gets larger.

A 2008 report issued by the British Library and the Joint Information Systems Committee backs that up...

"Deep log studies show that, from undergraduates to professors, people exhibit a strong tendency toward shallow, horizontal, 'flicking' behaviour in digital libraries. Society is **dumbing down**."

But does flicking necessarily mean we're dumbing down?

Are we thinking badly now, or just **differently**?

Educator Kate Hayles suggests that we're shifting our "cognitive styles" from **deep attention** to **hyper attention** in response to our zippy, info-rich age.

"Deep attention ... is characterized by concentrating on a single object for long periods, ignoring outside stimuli ... and having a high tolerance for long focus times."

"Hyper attention is characterized by switching focus rapidly ... preferring multiple information streams, seeking a high level of stimulation, and having a low tolerance for boredom."

Hayles suggests that this is a natural adaptation. Does that mean this Grand Theft Auto kid represents the **future of humanity**?

In **2004**, the National Endowment for the Arts released a study that found **fewer than half** of Americans read literature. It blamed the prevalence and passivity fostered by TV, radio, recordings, video games, and the Internet.

Back in 2002, when the 2004 survey data was collected, the Internet was far less interactive, far less rich... a relative **infant**.

But now reading, even among young digital natives, is sharply up!
And they read -- BOOKS!

OBVIOUSLY, *PEOPLE* MAKE *THINGS*, but less obviously, *things* also *make* people. The idea that humans and their tools "co-evolved" is now widely accepted by anthropologists.

When we started walking on two legs our brains grew a lot bigger. Many scientists believe we started walking on two legs *after* we started picking up clubs to hunt and defend ourselves.

We needed hands to carry clubs. So those who could balance on two legs prospered. The tools came first. Then bipedalism, bigger brains, nimbler hands, and smaller teeth.

Our tools changed our bodies and our brains.

Brain studies suggest that consuming information on the Internet develops different cognitive abilities, so it's likely we are being rewired now in response to our technology. That process doesn't stop. *It can't stop.*

And even the most strident critics of the Internet cannot truly wish for it stop, considering how far we have come since we grasped that first tool.

HUMANITY WILL NOT BE TOMORROW WHAT IT IS TODAY.

But that doesn't mean we can't reap some benefits today.

Gary Small of the Semel Institute for Neuroscience and Human Behavior at UCLA found that when computer-literate adults were asked to do a simple Internet search, their brains showed a higher level of activity than inexperienced computer users, lighting up all over the place.

In fact, the MRI study found twice as much brain activity in the Web-savvy group, in areas of the brain that control decision making and complex reasoning. And all the people in the study were elder adults, so it wasn't generational.

It seems Google wasn't making them stupid. If the scans measure anything, it was making them smarter.

I, ROBOT

On April 1, 2009, biomedical engineer Adam Wilson posted to Twitter by using a cap with sensors that could read his brainwaves.

Look, Ma! **No hands!**

TWITTER

U·S·I·N·G
E·E·G T·O
S·E·N·D
T·W·E·E·T

But that cap was ... unsightly. So scientists are developing ways to reach the Web using **invisible** brain implants.

Intel Corporation predicts it will succeed by 2020.

intel inside

Polymer nanotubes and silk fiber electrodes are easier on brain tissue than metal -- opening paths to cures for Parkinson's, epilepsy, blindness, deafness, paralysis, as well as the **enhancement** of **normal** brain function.

It also offers fresh meat to **mischief-makers.** Hacker vandals could remotely hijack or control neural devices, just as they infect computers with worms and viruses.

Heh-heh!

Humans determine whether their machines do more harm than good.

As the sage once said...

It is man who is the content of and the message of the media, **which are extensions of himself.**

MEDIUM = MESSAGE

—Marshall McLuhan

Electronic man must know the effects of the world he has made above all things.

Funny story: in the early 1900s, America quickly constructed its telephone network through little companies and cooperatives.

After the Russian Revolution, the Kremlin **could** have invested in telephones.

РОДИНА-МАТЬ ЗОВЕТ!

Instead it developed the **loudspeaker**.

Another perfect marriage of politics and media. One nation chooses the **chaos** of **one-to-one** communication; another, the **order** of **one-to-many**. Now we're blazing trails into the borderless territory of **many-to-many**.

But as the real and virtual merge in cyberspace, many technically savvy people fear we risk our individuality, our autonomy, our very **humanity**. As George Dyson wrote in "Darwin Among the Machines"...

In the game of life and evolution there are three players at the table: human beings, nature, and machines. I am firmly on the side of nature.

But nature, I suspect, is on the side of the machines.

When will the real and the virtual **merge**? In **2045**, says visionary inventor Ray Kurzweil. He calls that transition the **Singularity**.

What used to fit in a building now fits in your pocket, and what fits in your pocket today will fit inside a blood cell in 25 years ... We'll be able to send millions of nanobots -- blood cell - sized devices -- into our bloodstream...

They'll repair our bodies ... put our brains on the Internet ... and provide full-immersion virtual reality from within the nervous system. We'll become a hybrid of biological and non-biological intelligence.

By 2045, we'll have multiplied the overall intelligence of the human - machine civilization a billionfold. ... We will gain power over our fates. Our mortality will be in our own hands.

Many ... focus on what they perceive as a **loss** of some vital aspect of our **humanity**. To me, the essence of being human is not our limitations...

...it's our ability to reach **beyond** our limitations... We didn't stay on the ground. We didn't even stay on the planet. And we are already not **settling** for the limitations of our biology.

That's crazy!

And yet a lot of your predictions pan out. Like back in the '80s -- you correctly predicted the **moment** we'd have the World Wide Web...

And we'll get to the world of 2045 in thousands of little steps ... each step ... a new product that starts out not working that well, then it works a little better ... until we reach the Singularity.

Virtual reality pioneer Jaron Lanier doesn't buy it. He likens belief in the Singularity to the **Rapture**, when true Christians will fly up to heaven before the Apocalypse.

And through the Singularity, a hope of an **afterlife** is available to the most fervent believers.

But in fact, **extinction** is on the minds of many such believers. Kurzweil himself gives the planet "a better than even chance of making it through." And he's a glass-half-full kind of guy.

Damn you to hell!

Famine could do us in, or plague, asteroid, or alien invasion. And of course we could do **ourselves** in, in ways ranging from global warming to nuclear war to a takeover by our own artificial intelligence.

Our decisions have consequences -- so how do we decide? In 1954, Abraham Maslow formulated his "hierarchy of needs."

But what if I get **stuck** between sex and self-esteem?

Self-actualization -- which includes such qualities as "tolerance" and "acceptance of facts" -- seems so **far away**.

Self-Actualization

Self-Esteem

Belongingness, Love, Sex

Safety & Security

LIFE: Air, Water, Food, Shelter . . .

...I, MEDIA

How can we ensure that our development as moral and social animals keeps pace with our rapidly evolving communications technology?

By playing an active role in our media consumption...

TAP TAP
TAP

...trusting reporters who demonstrate fairness and reliability over time, offering corrections when they get something wrong, and when we **care** enough -- reading the original documents they worked from.

DATA.GOV

When we care really **intensely**... we can assemble in networks of peers and then draw attention to unreported information.

TOUCH SCREEN

CAST VOTE

As when, in 2003, documents posted by concerned "netizens" ultimately forced the makers of Diebold voting machines to change some of their practices.

Or in 2009, when protestors in post-election Tehran captured the world's attention by posting cell phone images and video of a young woman's death in the street.

Neda forever

People who assemble in spontaneous networks, whether around a funny video or a cataclysmic issue, can actually attract and engage more people than mass media with its built-in compromises, says Harvard's Yochai Benkler.

It begins with the **opposite** of lowest common denominator.

It begins with what irks you ... **individually**, the most.

After Matisse.

But I don't want to assemble. It's hard enough just being honest with myself. I'd actually like to get a leg up on Maslow's pyramid.

But for that, I need to learn from history and literature and art. I need open access to information...

...and that means less restrictive intellectual property laws...

...and an open Internet where people can freely invent and share their inventions. Any company that offers cool devices -- but bans applications that might offend some users -- stands in the way of evolution.

Worrying about offending people drags us back to the lowest common denominator.

Journalist Robert Wright believes that technology, especially information technology, paved the way from barbarism to global civilization -- but...

Technology ... is no guarantor of moral progress or civility.

Some scholars equate the origin of "civilization" with **writing**: writing equals Greece equals Plato; illiteracy equals barbarism equals Attila the Hun.

But if you add literacy to Attila the Hun, you don't get Plato.

You get **Genghis Khan.** He had the fastest large-scale information-processing technology of his era...

Nevertheless, Wright believes that technology has given us new opportunities to profit from one another's progress.

So it's not inevitable that we must always battle over a finite pie of possibilites.

Instead, we are able to play increasingly complex and wide-ranging **"non-zero-sum games"** -- to **collaborate** -- instead of always waging "I win - you lose" battles for primacy and resources...

As a result we become embedded in **larger and richer webs of interdependence.** It started happening at least as early as 15,000 years ago until, voilà! Here we are -- living in a global village.

To some people, the current era has the aura of a threshold; it has that unsettling, out-of-control feeling... Our species seems to face a kind of **test**...

...a test of political imagination -- but also a test of **moral imagination**.

So how will we do on this test?

Judging by history, the current turbulence will eventually yield to ... a new equilibrium, at a level of organization higher than any past equilibrium.

On the other hand, we could blow up the world.

It's true. With unlimited access to information, we have the power to collapse time and space, probe the most enduring mysteries, and maybe... blow up the world.

Neil Postman once observed that back when we had only newspapers, "news" was information we could **use** and **act** on locally.

The Tribune
RAINY WEATHER

Postman says the moment we could get instant news from everywhere -- news not directly **relevant** to us -- that's when news became **entertainment**.

The Tribune
RUNAWAY BRIDE

Or as G. K. Chesterton put it: Journalism largely consists of saying "Lord Jones is Dead" to people who never knew that Lord Jones was alive.

But Chesterton's news came from **newspapers**. In fact, as far back as Caesar's Acta Diurna, news has **always** been entertainment.

ACTA DIVRNA
CALIGVLA
CVTS VP

The difference between their eras and our own is that now, news from everywhere is relevant. Unemployment in the Middle East, environmental policies in Asia, epidemics in Africa -- this news affects us **all**.

And now we **can** act, easily, to spread the news, and even influence how those stories end.

HELP
Famine Relief

I'm Brooke Gladstone and I'm a reporter.

Hello, Brooke.

I am generally a dark individual, but I think this is a great time to be alive.

Our limits are purely human.

Our enemies are not the digital bits that dance across our screens but the neural impulses that animate our lizard brains.

ACKNOWLEDGMENTS

I WANTED TO WRITE A COMIC BOOK long before I wanted to write a book about the media. I thought writing in bubbles would be easier, more like radio. It *was* more like radio, but it wasn't easier.

Often, I was reminded that a *narrative* was crucial for graphic nonfiction. The most successful books were memoirs, histories, or journalism that traced events. Graphic nonfiction was not a suitable genre for a book about ideas, because ideas are hard to convey without a lot of words. It became a puzzle I wanted to solve. And if I did, it is because of the people mentioned below.

I received pivotal words of wisdom from Paul Auster, Alex Epstein, Dan Frank, Siri Hustvedt, Rafe Sagalyn, Art Speigelman, and Mark Stamaty; editorial suggestions from Lisa Gladstone, Mark Harelik, and Alissa Quart; and emotional sustenance from Deb Amos, Nancy Davis, Rick Davis, Stacey Gladstone, Peter Pringle, Eleanor Randolph, and Karen Trott.

Chris Maiurro and Joan Hilty were crucial in crafting an earlier incarnation of this project. Anaheed Alani meticulously fact-checked. I didn't always make the changes she suggested (conflicting sources) so whatever is still wrong is my fault.

I owe a great debt to the staff of *On the Media* and WNYC for their patience and support during the writing process, especially Dean Cappello, Alex Goldman, Ellen Horne, Dylan Keefe, Jennifer Munson, Mark Phillips, Megan Ryan, Nazanin Rafsanjani, Mike Vuolo, Jamie York, P. J. Vogt, and Laura Walker.

A thousand salaams to my cohost, old friend, and evil twin, Bob Garfield—and to my protector, commander, cheerleader, mother confessor, and senior producer, Katya Rogers.

Agent Jim Rutman (a fearsome basketball player) caught this project as it was bouncing down the court and deftly helped to spin a very weird proposal into a project that would play.

It landed at Norton, where it reaped the benefits of a talented, committed editorial, design, and marketing team (which deserves its sterling rep among writers) with editor Tom Mayer as point guard. Or playmaker. Enough with this metaphor.

I highly recommend the brilliant Tom Mayer for difficult projects that have no real comparables in the book biz. (I'm sure he'll thank me for that, right?) He made this book possible by adroitly balancing risk-taking with clarity, not to mention skillfully wrangling *two* creators. Which brings me to Josh Neufeld.

The difference between an illustrated text and one done "graphic" style in panels is that in the first case the pictures support the text, but in the second case they *replace* the text. "This is your book," Josh Neufeld explained. "You think up the pictures." Poor Josh. Miraculous Josh.

"Hey, Josh. Here's a link to an incredibly complicated print by Hogarth. Draw something like that, but have the people reading newspapers with these mastheads, okay?"

And that was a relatively easy panel. Josh was obliged to give this opinionated novice a crash course in what was possible in the genre. Still, I asked for the impossible and then watched him do it. I can't believe my luck.

Many people depicted in this book, and many more whose work is cited in the chapter notes, deserve credit for the ideas reflected in these pages. There are two others whose names appear nowhere that I want to single out: Scott McCloud, whose magisterial work *Understanding Comics* was the inspiration for *The Influencing Machine.* And the artist Terry Winters, whose lithograph "The Influencing Machine" (made in collaboration with the novelist Ben Marcus and printed by ULAE) sent me on my train of thought and supplied me with the title. If this book does well, *I will buy that print.*

There are Sophie and Maxine Kaplan, my daughters, two writers, two tough-minded realists with great discrimination and generous spirits, who vetted much of the text, kept me from foundering, and saved me from embarrassment time and again.

And finally, there is Fred Kaplan, who makes all things possible for me. Just about everything I have accomplished in my life can be traced back to him. I don't want to get too icky here. So I'll just say, Fred, I acknowledge you with all my heart.

—BROOKE GLADSTONE

WHEN THE PHONE RANG TWO YEARS AGO and I recognized the voice of the woman on the other end—from my radio!—I had no idea what lay in store. The caller was Brooke Gladstone, from one of my favorite NPR shows, *On the Media*. As both an NPR and a media junkie, I jumped at the chance to work with Brooke on her "media manifesto in comic book form." As much as I looked forward to crafting the images, I looked forward even more to learning about the subject from such a brilliant and original thinker. And it's been a memorable collaboration—thrilling, heady, educational, sometimes frustrating, and, ultimately, extremely satisfying. Thank you, Brooke: I wouldn't trade the last two years for anything.

Editor Tom Mayer bought into our vision of the book from day one, and his energy and patience never wavered. Not only did he juggle two opinionated, strong-willed creators, but he always managed it with aplomb.

Agent Kate Lee continues to be what every author needs: a great listener, an enthusiastic supporter, and a much-needed reality check—in other words, a real friend. Brooke has already thanked Jim Rutman, who really was a perfect guide through the project's initial phases.

This book owes a real debt to Randy Jones and Susann Ferris-Jones. Their willingness to step in at the last minute to help the book make its deadline—and their ability to pull it off— gives new meaning to "keeping up with the Joneses"! And their patience and good humor were icing on the cake. Similar kudos go to Nick Micciola, Echo Eggebrecht, and Matt Alloman— without them this book would never have made it to the finish line.

Designers Mark Melnick and Neil Swaab, production manager Anna Oler, editorial assistant Denise Scarfi, and publicist Jessica Purcell have also performed above and beyond the call.

Sari Wilson is my teacher, my inspiration, my sounding board, my drill instructor—and my best friend. She's the reason I was able to sit at my drawing table and stay there until the job was done. I try to tell her every day, and it's no secret from anyone else who knows me—I love her with all my heart.

—JOSH NEUFELD

·

SOURCES

Most of the quotations in this book and much of the thematic material were taken from a variety of sources. When the sources are not directly cited in the text, the books, articles, and other media that I consulted appear below largely in the order they are first reflected. Obviously some works have greater and repeated resonance and so should, by all rights, appear more than once. That seemed needlessly repetitive and complicated so I haven't done that.

INTRODUCTION

pp. xv–xvi: Mike Jay, *The Air Loom Gang: The Strange and True Story of James Tilly Matthews and his Visionary Madness* (New York: Basic Books, 2004*)*.

pp. xvii–xix: Victor Tausk, *"On the Origin of the 'Influencing Machine' in Schizophrenia."* He wrote it in 1919. It was first published in 1933, in the journal *Psychoanalytic Quarterly* 2: 519–56.

p. xix, panel 2: Rochelle G. K. Kainer, *The Collapse of the Self: And Its Therapeutic Restoration* (London: Analytic Press, 1999).

p. xxii, panels 1–3: Walter Lippmann, *Public Opinion* (New York: Harcourt, Brace, 1922).

p. xxii, panel 6: John Dewey, widely quoted, as in Laurence J. Peter, ed., *Peter's Quotations: Ideas for Our Times.*(New York: HarperCollins, 1993).

p. xxii, panel 7: *Ultimate Spider-Man, Vol. 1: Power and Responsibility* (New York: Marvel Comics, 2002).

IN THE BEGINNING

pp. 3–4: The Guatemala example is drawn from my interview with archaeologist Kevin Johnston, *On the Media,* NPR, July 28, 2001.

pp. 5–6: Information on the *Acta Diurna* is drawn from C. Anthony Giffard, "Ancient Rome's Daily Gazette," *Journalism History* (Winter 1975–76): 106–9.

p. 7: Mitchell Stephens, "History of Newspapers," *Collier's Encyclopedia* (New York: Collier's, 1995).

p. 7, panel 2: Illustration after William Hogarth, *Beer Street and Gin Lane* (1751).

p. 8, panel 1: **Poet John Milton's polemical tract against** censorship, *Areopagitica*, was published on November 23, 1644. It is widely available online.

THE AMERICAN EXCEPTION

p. 9: Trial record from John Peter Zenger, *A Brief Narrative of the Case and Trial of John Peter Zenger* (1736), reprinted by University of Missouri–Kansas City School of Law at http://www.law.umkc .edu/.

pp. 11-12: Paul Starr, *The Creation of the Media: Political Origins of Modern Communications* (New York: Basic Books, 2004).

p. 11: Timothy E. Cook, *Governing with the News: The News Media as a Political Thought* (Chicago: University of Chicago Press, 1998).

pp. 11–14: Geoffrey R. Stone, *Perilous Times: Free Speech in Wartime from the Sedition Act of 1798 to the War on Terrorism* (New York: W. W. Norton, 2004).

p. 14 and p. 18: Andrew Lipscomb and Albert Ellergy Bergh, eds., *The Writings of Thomas Jefferson* (Washington DC: Thomas Jefferson Memorial Association, 1903–4).

pp. 15–17: Eric Burns, *Infamous Scribblers: The Founding Fathers and the Rowdy Beginnings of American Journalism* (New York: PublicAffairs, 2006).

p. 16, panel 1: Illustration adapted from a portrait of Samuel Adams by John Singleton Copley (1772).

p. 17: Interview with Eric Burns, *On the Media,* NPR, June 2, 2006.

EXISTENTIAL ANGST

pp. 22–26: Stone, *Perilous Times.*

pp. 24–25: Victor S. Navasky, *Naming Names* (New York: Viking Press, 1980).

p. 27, panel 1: Daniel Ellsberg, *Secrets: A Memoir of Vietnam and the Pentagon Papers* (New York: Viking, 2002).

p. 28, panel 1: Meeting of President Nixon, H. R. Haldeman, and Ronald Ziegler, 2:42–3:33 p.m., June 17, 1971, National Security Archive, http://www.gwu .edu/~nsarchiv/NSAEBB/NSAEBB48/nixon.html.

p. 28, panel 4: Statement of Justice Hugo Black concurring in *New York Times v. United States* (1971).

p. 29, panel 3: Chris Mooney, "Back to Church," *American Prospect*, November 5, 2001.

p. 30: U.S. House of Representatives Committee on Government Reform, Special Investigations Division, "Secrecy in the Bush Administration," September 14, 2004, prepared by Rep. Henry A. Waxman.

p. 31: Charles Lewis and Mark Reading-Smith, "False Pretences" (article summarizing the misstatements of the George W. Bush White House, written for the Center for Public Integrity, Washington DC), January 23, 2008.

p. 32, panels 1–2: Remarks by the President in Welcoming Senior Staff and Cabinet Secretaries to the White House, January 21, 2009. Click on the "briefing" tab on the home page of www.whitehouse.gov.

p. 32, panel 3: "President Obama keeping secret locations of coal ash sites," Associated Press, June 12, 2009.

p. 32, panel 4: Bob Egelko, "Government Opts for Secrecy in Wiretap Suit," *San Francisco Chronicle*, April 7, 2009.

p. 33, panel 2: Ronald Reagan, speech, December 8, 1987, at http://www.youtube.com/watch?v=As6y5eI01XE.

p. 33, panel 3: *I. F. Stone's Weekly*, August 3, 1967.

p. 33, panel 4: Alfred Denning in *The Road to Justice* (1988) suggests that the quote is misattributed to Jefferson, that it in fact originates with Irish politician John Philpot Curran in a speech upon the Right of Election (1790): "It is the common fate of the indolent to see their rights become a prey to the active. The condition upon which God hath given liberty to man is eternal vigilance; which condition if he break, servitude is at once the consequence of his crime and the punishment of his guilt."

p. 34, panel 4: Edward R. Murrow on *See it Now*, CBS, March 9, 1954.

CANIS JOURNALISTICUS

p. 35, panel 1: Arthur Schopenhauer, *The Art of Literature,* translated by T. Bailey Saunders (Mineola, NY: Courier Dover Publications, 2004). I cite a commonly used paraphrase. In Saunders's translation it goes: "… all journalists are, in the nature of their calling, alarmists; and this is their way of giving interest to what they write. Herein they are like little dogs; if anything stirs, they immediately set up a shrill bark."

p. 35, panel 2: Henrik Ibsen, widely quoted, as in Colin Jarman, *The Book of Poisonous Quotes* (New York: McGraw-Hill Professional, 1993), 232.

p. 35, panel 3: William Butler Yeats, letter to Katharine Tynan, August 30, 1888, Houghton Library, Harvard College Library, Cambridge, MA.

p. 35, panel 4: Bobby Fischer, widely quoted, as in "Bobby Fischer: The Greatest Chess Player of Them All?" *The Independent on Sunday,* January 19, 2008.

p. 37, panel 1: The composition and some of the illustrations in this panel pay homage to Alan Moore and Dave Gibbons's *Watchmen* (1987).

p. 37, panel 1: Pew Research Center for the People and the Press, Project for Excellence in Journalism, Local TV News Project 2002: "How Strong is the Case for Quality?" November 1, 2002.

p. 37, panel 3: Pew Research Center, "Press Accuracy Rating Hits Two-Decade Low: Public Evaluations of the News Media: 1985–2009," September 13, 2009.

p. 38: Interviews with Helen Thomas, *On the Media,* NPR, January 6, 2001, and July 18, 2003.

p. 39: Albert Camus, *Resistance, Rebellion and Death* (New York: Modern Library, 1963), 75.

p. 39: Meeting of President Nixon, H. R. Haldeman, and Ronald Ziegler, 2:42–3:33 p.m., June 17, 1971,

National Security Archive, http://www.gwu.edu/
~nsarchiv/NSAEBB/NSAEBB48/nixon.html.

p. 40, panel 1: Cartoon, *Life,* no date given, drawn from
an archive at the University of Texas, http://viz.cwrl
.utexas.edu/files/watertoon.jpg. This cartoon was
found in the online archive of the Jim Crow Museum
of Ferris State University. The webmaster explained
that it was found, cut out, and placed with pre-1920s
cartoons from *Life* magazine, thus it was attributed
to *Life,* more or less by association. We could find no
clear confirmation of the periodical or date.

p. 40, panel 2: Sean Delonas, cartoon, *New York Post,*
February 18, 2009.

p. 40, panels 3–4: "Afflicting the Afflicted: How Eight
U.S. Newspaper Editorial Pages Responded to the
1942 Japanese Internment," submitted to the AEJMC
History Division as part of the Association for
Education in Journalism and Mass Communication
annual convention, Washington DC, August 5–8,
2001.

p. 41, panel 1: Anderson Cooper interview with Mary
Landrieu, CNN, September 1, 2005.

p. 41, panel 2: Tim Russert interview with Homeland
Security Secretary Michael Chertoff, *Meet the Press,*
NPR, September 4, 2005.

p. 41, panel 3: Fox's Shepard Smith with National Guard
troops, cited in Howard Kurtz, "At Last, Reporters'
Feelings Rise to the Surface," *Washington Post,*
September 5, 2005.

p. 42, panel 1: New Orleans Mayor C. Ray Nagin, *Oprah,*
September 6, 2005; Jim Caviezel with Miles O'Brian,
CNN, September 11, 2005; John Gibson, Fox News,
September 1, 2005.

p. 42, panel 2: Susannah Rosenblatt and James Rainey,
"Katrina Takes a Toll on Truth," *Los Angeles Times,*
September 27, 2005.

BIRDS ON A WIRE

p. 43, panel 1: Charles Gibson and Diane Sawyer, *Good
Morning America*, ABC, September 11, 2001.

p. 43, panel 2: *The O'Reilly Factor,* Fox News, December
18, 2007.

p. 43, panel 3: David Barstow, "Behind TV Analysts,
Pentagon's Hidden Hand," *New York Times,* April 20,
2008; David Barstow, "One Man's Military-Industrial-
Media Complex," *New York Times,* November 29, 2008.

p. 44, panel 1: Collage of *New York Times* headlines in the
run-up to the 2003 U.S. invasion of Iraq.

p. 45: Interview with Walter Pincus, *On the Media,* NPR,
September 19, 2003.

p. 45: Ari Berman, "The Postwar Post," *The Nation,*
September 17, 2003.

p. 46: Interview with Scott Armstrong, *On the Media,*
NPR, May 28, 2004.

NEWS YOU CAN'T USE

p. 47: A banner headline "Dewey Defeats Truman" ran
across the front page of the *Chicago Daily Tribune,*
November 3, 1948.

p. 48: Interview with David Moore, *On The Media,* NPR,
September 5, 2008.

p. 48: These polls were all conducted in the first week of
May 2008: *Times/*Bloomberg: McCain 40%, Obama
46%; *USA Today/*Gallup: McCain 48%, Obama 47%;
CBS: McCain 38%, Obama 50%; Rasmussen: McCain
47%, Obama 43%.

pp. 49–51: The "Goldilocks Number" adapted from
"Prime Number," *On the Media,* NPR, July 30, 2010.

p. 52, panel 2: Mark Twain, "Petrified Man," *Virginia City
Territorial Enterprise*, October 4, 1862.

p. 52, panels 3–4: Mark Twain, "My First Lie and How
I Got Out of It," *The Man that Corrupted Hadleyburg*
(Fairfield, IA: 1st World Library—Literary Society,
2004).

p. 53, panel 2–3: Eric Burns, *All the News Unfit to Print:
How Things Were . . . and How They Were Reported*
(Hoboken, NJ: Wiley, 2009).

p. 53, panel 4: W. Joseph Campbell, *Yellow Journalism,
Puncturing the Myths, Defining the Legacies* (Westport,
CT: Praeger, 2001).

p. 54, panel 2: "Border Insecurity: Deadly Imports," *Lou
Dobbs Tonight,* CNN, April 13, 2005.

p. 54, panel 3: *Sixty Minutes,* CBS, May 6, 2007.

p. 54, panel 4: David Leonhardt, "Truth, Fiction and Lou
Dobbs," *New York Times,* May 30, 2007.

p. 56: Interview with Philip Knightley, *On The Media,*
NPR, March 21, 2003.

THE GREAT REFUSAL

p. 57, panel 2: Illustration after Gustave Doré, *Dante at the
Gates of Hell* (1861–68).

p. 57, panel 2: Dante Alighieri, *Inferno,* Canto III, lines
59–60.

p. 57, panel 3: Evan Thomas, *Robert Kennedy: His Life*
(New York: Simon and Schuster, 2002), 22.

p. 59: W. B. Yeats, "The Second Coming" (1921), in *The Collected Poems of W. B. Yeats* (New York: Scribner, 1996).

BIAS

p. 60, panel 2: Transcript and video of Sulzberger's speech are available at the C-Span video archive, http://www.c-spanvideo.org/program/UNY.

p. 60, panel 3: Rush Limbaugh, widely quoted, as in "A Case In Point: Doublespeak—From the Horse's Mouth" (opinion piece), *San Francisco Chronicle*, May 10, 2009.

p. 61: Study conducted by the Center for Media and Public Affairs at George Mason University, released January 25, 2010.

p. 62, panels 1–3: George Eliot (Mary Ann Evans), *Middlemarch: A Study of Provincial Life* (New York: Harper & Brothers, 1873), 70.

p. 63, panels 1–2: William Samuelson and Richard Zeckhauser, "Status Quo Bias in Decision Making," *Journal of Risk and Uncertainty* 1, no. 1 (March 1988).

p. 63, panel 4: Andrew R. Cline, PhD, "A Better Understanding of Media Bias," Rhetorica.net.

p. 63, panel 5: *Time* magazine cover, November 20, 2000.

p. 64: Eason Jordan, "The News We Kept to Ourselves," *New York Times*, December 4, 2009.

p. 65, panel 1: Dana Priest and Barton Gellman, "U.S. Decries Abuse but Defends Interrogations 'Stress and Duress' Tactics Used on Terrorism Suspects Held in Secret Overseas Facilities," *Washington Post,* December 26, 2002.

p. 66, panels 2–3: "Sen. John McCain Attacks Pat Robertson, Jerry Falwell, Republican Establishment as Harming GOP Ideals," CNN, February 28, 2000.

pp. 67–68: Peter Maass, "The Toppling: How the media inflated a minor moment in a long war," *The New Yorker*, January 10, 2011.

p. 69: Andrea Stone, "Fog of War, Partisanship Cloud Kerry's Vietnam Record," *USA Today,* August 19, 2004; Fairness and Accuracy in Media, media advisory: "Swift Boat Smears Press Corps Keeps Anti-Kerry Distortions Alive," August 30, 2004; "Republican-Funded Group Attacks Kerry's War Record," FactCheck.org, updated August 22, 2004; Eric Boehlert, *Lapdogs: How the Press Rolled Over for Bush* (New York: Free Press, 2006).

p. 70: *Scientific American*, April 1, 2005.

WAR

p. 71: World War One—era illustration adapted from Committee on Public Information (CPI) propaganda poster.

p. 71: Carl von Clausewitz, *On War*, Book 2, Chapter 2, "Third Attribute: Uncertainty of All Information." Edited and translated by Michael Howard and Peter Paret (Princeton: Princeton University Press, 1976).

p. 72: Sheldon Rampton and John Clyde Stauber, *Weapons of Mass Deception: The Uses of Propaganda in Bush's War on Iraq* (New York: Penguin, 2003), 72–80.

p. 72: Chris Hedges, *War Is a Force that Gives Us Meaning* (New York: PublicAffairs, 2002).

p. 73: Phillip Knightley, *The First Casualty: The War Correspondent as Hero and Myth-Maker from the Crimea to Kosovo* (Baltimore: Johns Hopkins University Press, 2002). I return to this book again and again in this chapter.

p. 74, panel 2: Wilbur Storey, editor-in-chief, *Chicago Times*, widely quoted, as in Stephen Bates, *If No News, Send Rumors: Anecdotes of American Journalism* (New York: Henry Holt & Co., 1991). Meanwhile, historian W. Joseph Campbell in a recent paper "'Severe in Invective': Franc Wilkie, Wilbur Storey, and the improbable 'send rumors'," published by the Association for Education in Journalism and Mass Communication, offers impressive evidence to dispute the truth of the quote.

p. 74, panel 3: *Richmond Enquirer*, July 10, 1863.

p. 75: *Harper's Weekly*, October 31, 1863. Illustration adapted from Theodore P. Davis, "The Army of the Cumberland Rebel Attack Upon Wagons in Anderson Gap," published in *Harper's Weekly* (1863).

p. 76: Steven W. Sears, "The First News Blackout," *American Heritage*, June–July 1985.

p. 77, panel 1: Illustration adapted from *Battle of Antietam—Army of the Potomac: Gen. Geo. B. McClellan, comm., Sept. 17, 1862* (Kurz & Allison, 1888).

p. 77: George W. Smalley, *New York Tribune*, September 19, 1862.

p. 78: Bill Kovach, "Out of the Pool!," *New York Times,* September 23, 2001.

p. 79: Aaron Delwiche, "Of Fraud and Force Fast Woven: Domestic Propaganda During The First World War," FirstWorldWar.com.

p. 79, panel 5: George Creel (1947) quoted in Robin K. Krumm, Major USAF, "Information Warfare: An Air

Force Policy for the Role of Public Affairs," School of Advanced Airpower Studies, 1996–97.

pp. 80–81: George Seldes, "One Man's Newspaper Game," *Freedom of the Press* (Garden City, NY: Garden City Publishing Co., 1937), 31–37; George Seldes, *You Can't Print That!: The Truth Behind the News 1918–1928* (Garden City, NY: Garden City Publishing Co., 1929); George Seldes, *Witness to a Century: Encounters with the Noted, the Notorious, and the Three SOBs* (New York: Ballantine Books, 1987).

p. 81, panel 3: "Stab in the Back" illustration adapted from an Austrian postcard (1919).

p. 82: Phillip Seib, *Broadcasts from the Blitz: How Edward R. Murrow Helped Lead America Into War* (Dulles, VA: Potomac Books, 2006).

p. 82: George Roeder Jr., *The Censored War: American Visual Experience During World War Two* (New Haven: Yale University Press, 1995); Michael S. Sweeney, *Secrets of Victory: The Office of Censorship and the American Press and Radio in World War II* (Chapel Hill: University of North Carolina Press, 2000).

p. 83, panel 1: Ernie Pyle, "The God-Damned Infantry," May 22, 1943, Scripps-Howard newspaper chain.

p. 83, panel 2: Ernie Pyle, "On Victory In Europe," unpublished column, Indiana University School of Journalism.

p. 83, panels 3–4: Greg Mitchell, "The Press and Hiroshima: August 6, 1945," *Editor and Publisher*, August 5, 2005.

p. 84: Robert J. Lifton and Greg Mitchell, *Hiroshima in America* (New York: Harper Perennial, 1995); Mark Selden, "Nagasaki 1945: While Independents Were Scorned, Embed Won Pulitzer," 2005, YaleGlobal Online, http://yaleglobal.yale.edu, a publication of the Yale Center for the Study of Globalization.

p. 85, panels 1–3: Anthony Weller, *First into Nagasaki: George Weller's Censored Eyewitness Dispatches on the Atomic Bombing and Japan's POWs* (New York: Three Rivers Press, 2007).

p. 85, panel 2: Wilfred Burchett, "The Atomic Plague," *Daily Express*, September 5, 1945.

p. 85, panel 4: David Goodman, "Keeping Secrets," *On the Media*, NPR, August 5, 2005.

p. 86, panels 4–5: John Hersey, "Hiroshima," *The New Yorker*, August 31, 1946.

p. 86, panel 6: John Hersey interviewed by Jonathan Dee, *Paris Review* (Summer–Fall 1986).

p. 87: Daniel C. Hallin, *The "Uncensored War": The Media and Vietnam* (New York: Oxford University Press, 1986). This book frequently informed my discussion of Vietnam.

p. 87, panels 1–3: Peter Brush, "What Really Happened at Cam Ne," Historynet.com. Brush, a Marine veteran who participated in the battle of Khe Sanh, is a librarian at Vanderbilt University in Nashville, TN.

p. 87, panel 4: David Halberstam, *The Powers That Be* (New York: Knopf, 1979).

p. 89, panels 3–4: Ronald Reagan, "Peace: Restoring the Margin of Safety," speech at Veterans of Foreign Wars convention, Chicago, IL, August 18, 1980.

p. 90: William M. Hammond, *Public Affairs: The Military and The Media, 1962–1968* (Washington DC: U.S. Army Center of Military History, 1988).

p. 90: James J. Wirtz, *The Tet Offensive: Intelligence Failure in War* (Ithaca, NY: Cornell University Press, 1991).

p. 91: Jim Naureckas, "Gulf War Coverage: The Worst Censorship Was at Home," *EXTRA!* Special Gulf War Issue, 1991, Fairness and Accuracy in Reporting, http://www.fair.org/index.php?page=1518.

p. 91: Michael Morgan, Justin Lewis, and Sut Jhally, "The Gulf War: A Study of the Media, Public Opinion, and Public Knowledge," Center for the Study of Communication, University of Massachusetts, 1991.

p. 91: Malcolm W. Browne, "The Military vs. the Press," *New York Times*, March 3, 1991.

p. 92, panels 1–2: Jeffery Kahn, "Postmortem: Iraq War Media Coverage Dazzled But It Also Obscured," UC-Berkeley NewsCenter, March 18, 2004.

p. 92, panels 2–3: Project for Excellence in Journalism, "Embedded Reporters: What Are Americans Getting?" April 3, 2003.

p. 92, panels 3–4: Jack Shafer, "The PR War: The General who Devised the 'Embedded' Program Deserves a Fourth Star," *Slate,* March 25, 2003.

pp. 93–94: "The Embed Experiment," interviews with John Burnett, *On the Media*, NPR, March 21, 2008.

p. 95, panels 2–4: Michael Herr, *Dispatches* (New York: Knopf, 1977).

OBJECTIVITY

pp. 96–97: Michael Schudson, *Discovering the News: A Social History of American Newspapers* (New York: Basic Books, 1978).

p. 97, panel 4: Illustration after Stevens (artist) and Bobbett-Hooper (engraver), "Badgering Him," published in *Vanity Fair* (1860).

pp. 97–99: Michael Schudson, "The Emergence of the Objectivity Norm in American Journalism," in Michael Hechter and Karl-Dieter Opp, eds., *Social Norms* (New York: Russell Sage Foundation, 2001).

p. 98: Adolph S. Ochs, "An Editorial Voice," *New York Times*, August 18, 1896.

> To undertake the management of *The New-York Times*, with its great history for right doing, and to attempt to keep bright the lustre which Henry J. Raymond and George Jones have given it is an extraordinary task. But if a sincere desire to conduct a high-standard newspaper, clean, dignified, and trustworthy, requires honesty, watchfulness, earnestness, industry, and practical knowledge applied with common sense, I entertain the hope that I can succeed in maintaining the high estimate that thoughtful, pure-minded people have ever had of *The New-York Times*.
>
> It will be my earnest aim that *The New-York Times* give the news, all the news, in concise and attractive form, in language that is parliamentary in good society, and give it as early, if not earlier, than it can be learned through any other reliable medium; to give the news impartially, without fear or favor, regardless of party, sect, or interests involved; to make of the columns of The New-York Times a forum for the consideration of all questions of public importance, and to that end to invite intelligent discussion from all shades of opinion.
>
> There will be no radical changes in the personnel of the present efficient staff. Mr. Charles R. Miller, who has so ably for many years presided over the editorial pages, will continue to be the editor; nor will there be a departure from the general tone and character and policies pursued with relation to public questions that have distinguished *The New-York Times* as a non-partisan newspaper—unless it be, if possible, to intensify its devotion to the cause of sound money and tariff reform, opposition to wastefulness and peculation in administering public affairs, and in its advocacy of the lowest tax consistent with good government, and no more government than is absolutely necessary to protect society, maintain individual and vested rights, and assure the free exercise of a sound conscience.

p. 100, panel 1: Ernest Hemingway, *A Farewell to Arms* (New York: Charles Scribner's Sons, 1929).

p. 100, panel 2: Erich Maria Remarque, *All Quiet on the Western Front* (New York: Glencoe/McGraw-Hill, 2000), 6.

p. 100, panel 3: Wilfred Owen, "Dulce et Decorum Est," in *The Collected Poems of Wilfred Owen* (New York: New Directions, 1965).

p. 100, panel 4: Illustration after Marcel Duchamp, *L.H.O.O.Q.* (1919).

p. 100, panel 5: Tristan Tzara, "Dada Manifesto" (1918) and "Lecture on Dada" (1922), in *Seven Dada Manifestos and Lampisteries* (Edison, NJ: Riverrun Press, 1981).

p. 101, panel 1: Edward Bernays, *Propaganda* (New York: H. Liveright, 1928).

p. 101, panels 2–3: Larry Tye, *The Father of Spin: Edward L. Bernays and the Birth of Public Relations* (New York: Crown, 1998).

p. 101, panels 4–6: Walter Lippmann, *Liberty and the News* (1920; Charleston, SC: Forgotten Books, 2010).

pp. 102–3: David T. Z. Mindich, *Just the Facts: How "Objectivity" Came to Define American Journalism* (New York: New York University Press, 1998).

p. 104: Nancy E. Bernhard, *U.S. Television News and Cold War Propaganda, 1947–1960* (Cambridge: Cambridge University Press, 1999).

p. 104: Thomas Patrick Doherty, *Cold War, Cool Medium: Television, McCarthyism, and American Culture* (New York: Columbia University Press, 2003).

p. 105: Daniel C. Hallin, *We Keep America on Top of the World: Television Journalism and the Public Sphere* (New York: Routledge, 1993).

p. 106: "Senator Stone's Mistake," *New York Times*, July 30, 1909.

p. 107, panels 5–6: Pew Research Center for People and the Press, "Public Struggles with Possible War in Iraq," January 30, 2003.

pp. 108–9: "Journalists as People," *On the Media*, NPR, September 10, 2004.

DISCLOSURE

p. 112: Ida Minerva Tarbell, *The Tariff in Our Times* (New York: Macmillan, 1911).

p. 113: David Weinberger, "Transparency is the New Objectivity," *Journal of the Hyperlinked Organization,* www.hyperorg.com/blogger, July 19, 2009.

p. 114: James Poniewozik, "The Case for Full Disclosure," *Time*, March 13, 2008.

p. 115: Shanto Iyengar and Richard Morin, "Red Media, Blue Media: Evidence for a Political Litmus Test in Online News Readership," *Washington Post*, May 3, 2006.

THE MATRIX IN ME

p. 118: Lawrence E. Williams and John A. Bargh, "Experiencing Physical Warmth Promotes Interpersonal Warmth," *Science* 322, no. 5901 (October 24, 2008): 606–7.

p. 119: Chun Siong Soon, Marcel Brass, Hans-Jochen Heinze, and John-Dylan Haynes, "Unconscious Determinants of Free Decisions in the Human Brain," *Nature Neuroscience* (April 13, 2008), 543–45.

p. 120: Shankar Vedantam, *The Hidden Brain: How Our Unconscious Minds Elect Presidents, Control Markets, Wage Wars, and Save Our Lives* (New York: Spiegel and Grau, 2009).

p. 122, panels 5–8: Timothy C. Brock and Joe L. Balloun, "Behavioral Receptivity to Dissonant Information," *Journal of Personality and Social Psychology* 6, no. 4, pt.1 (August 1967): 413–28.

p. 123: "Debunk This!" *On the Media*, NPR, July 3, 2009.

p. 123: Norbert Schwarz, Lawrence J. Sanna, Ian Skurnik, and Carolyn Yoon, "Metacognitive Experiences and the Intricacies of Setting People Straight: Implications for Debiasing and Public Information Campaigns," *Advances in Experimental Social Psychology*, 39 (2007): 127–61.

p. 124, panel 1: Walt Whitman, "Song of Myself," in *The Complete Poems* (New York: Penguin, 2005).

pp. 124–25: Leon Festinger, Henry Riecken, and Stanley Schacter, *When Prophecy Fails: A Social and Psychological Study of a Modern Group that Predicted the Destruction of the World* (New York: HarperTorchbooks, 1956).

p. 126: Alan Baddeley, *Your Memory: A User's Guide* (Richmond Hill, Ont.: Firefly Books, 2004).

p. 127, panel 2: Farhad Manjoo, *True Enough: Learning to Live in a Post-Fact Society* (New York: Wiley, 2008).

p. 128: Illustration after Michelangelo, *Delphic Sibyl* (Sistine Chapel, 1510).

p. 128: "Choice," *Radiolab*, NPR, November 17, 2008.

p. 128: William James, *Pragmatism: A New Name for Some Old Ways of Thinking* (1907) in *Pragmatism and Other Writings* (New York: Penguin, 2000).

p. 128: James Fitzjames Stephen, *Liberty, Equality, Fraternity, and Three Brief Essays* (Chicago: University of Chicago Press, 1991), 271.

THE INFLUENCING MACHINES

p. 129: Miller McPherson, Lynn Smith-Lovin, and James M. Cook, "Homophily in Social Networks," *Annual Review of Sociology* 27 (August 2001): 415–44.

p. 130: Cass Sunstein, *Republic.com 2.0* (Princeton: Princeton University Press, 2007).

p. 131: Ron Callari, "Iris Recognition and Augmented Reality IDs Straight from 'Minority Report,'" InventorSpot.com, April 4, 2010.

p. 131: Babak A. Parviz, "Augmented Reality in a Contact Lens," *IEEE Spectrum,* September 2009.

p. 132: Nicholas Carr, "Is Google Making Us Stupid?: What the Internet Is Doing to our Brains," *Atlantic,* July/August 2008.

p. 133, panel 5: Brian Stelter, "Report Ties Children's Use of Media to Their Health," *New York Times*, December 2, 2008.

pp. 134–35: Vaughan Bell, "Don't Touch That Dial! A history of media technology scares, from the printing press to Facebook," Slate.com, February 15, 2010.

p. 135, panels 2–4: Tibor Braun, "Growth of the Literature and the Electronic Controllability Explosion: The Barnaby Rich Syndrome," Calsi .org, accessed at calsi.org/2007/wp-content/uploads/2007/11/tibor_braun.pdf; T. Braun and S. Zsindely, "Growth of Scientific Literature and the Barnaby Rich Effect," *Scientometrics* 7, nos. 3–6 (1985): 529–30.

p. 135, panel 5: Plato, *Phaedrus,* translated by Benjamin Jowett (Fairford, UK: Echo Library, 2006).

p. 136, panels 1–2: Douglas Adams, *The Salmon of Doubt: Hitchhiking the Galaxy One Last Time* (New York: Crown, 2002).

p. 136, panel 3: Douglas Adams, *The Hitchhiker's Guide to the Galaxy* (New York: Pocket Books, 1979), 27.

UM, PANIC?

p. 137, panels 1–2: Sheena S. Iyengar and Mark R. Lepper, "When Choice Is Demotivating: Can One Desire Too Much of a Good Thing?" *Journal of Personality and Social Psychology* 79, no. 6 (December 2000): 995–1006.

p. 137, panel 3: Benjamin Scheibehenne, Rainer Greifeneder, and Peter M. Todd, "Can There Ever Be Too Many Options? A Meta-Analytic Review of Choice Overload," *Journal of Consumer Research* 37, no. 3 (August 2010): 409–25.

p. 138: Russ Juskalian, "Overload!" (interview with Clay Shirky, part 1), *Columbia Journalism Review*, December 19, 2008.

p. 139: Miller McPherson, Lynn Smith-Lovin, and Matthew E. Brashears, "Social Isolation in America: Changes in Core Discussion Networks over Two Decades," *American Sociological Review* 71 (June 2006): 353–75.

pp. 139–40: Keith Hampton, Lauren Sessions, Eun Ja Her, and Lee Rainie, "Social Isolation and New Technology," Internet and American Life Project, Pew Research Center, November 4, 2009.

p. 140, panel 3: James Melkie, "Mother's phone call as comforting as a hug, says oxytocin study," *Guardian* (UK), May 12, 2010.

p. 141: Nicholas Carr, *The Shallows: What the Internet Is Doing to our Brains* (New York: W. W. Norton, 2010).

p. 141: Arnie Cooper, "Computing the Cost: Nicholas Carr on How the Internet Is Rewiring Our Brain," *Sun*, no. 399 (March 2009): 4–11.

p. 142, panels 1–3: Katherine Hayles, "Hyper and Deep Attention: The Generational Divide in Cognitive Modes," *Profession* (2007): 187–99.

p. 142, panel 4: "Reading at Risk: A Survey of Literary Reading in America Executive Summary," National Endowment for the Arts, June 2004.

p. 142, panel 6: "Reading on the Rise: A New Chapter in American Literacy," National Endowment for the Arts, January 2009.

p. 143: Milford H. Wolpoff, "Competitive Exclusion among Lower Pleistocene Hominids: The Single Species Hypothesis," *Man* 6 (1971): 602.

p. 143: Andrew Lock and Charles R. Peters, *Handbook of Human Symbolic Evolution* (Oxford: Blackwell, 1999), 144–46.

p. 144: "The Net Effect," *On the Media*, NPR, April 3, 2009.

I, ROBOT

p. 145, panel 1: Brandon Keim, "Twitter Telepathy: Researchers Turn Thoughts Into Tweets," Wired.com, April 20, 2009.

p. 145, panel 2: Sharon Gaudin, "Intel: Chips in Brains Will Control Computers by 2020," *Computerworld*, November 19, 2009.

p. 146, panel 1: Katherine Bourzac, "Brain Interfaces Made of Silk," *Technology Review*, April 19, 2010; "Conducting Polymer Nanotubes Take Us a Step Closer to Better Brain Implants," *Medical News Today*, September 30, 2009; Ivan S. Kotchetkov et al., "Brain-Computer Interfaces: Military, Neurosurgical, and Ethical Perspective," *Journal of Neurosurgery* 28, no. 5 (May 2010); Hadley Leggett, "The Next Hacking Frontier: Your Brain?" *Wired Science*, July 9, 2009; Donald Melanson, "British scientist becomes first human 'infected' with a computer virus," *Engadget*, May 26, 2010.

p. 146, panel 2: Marshall McLuhan, *Take Today: The Executive as Dropout* (New York: Harcourt Brace Jovanovich, 1972).

p. 147, panels 1–2: Paul Starr, *The Creation of the Media* (New York: Basic Books, 2005).

p. 147, panel 3: George Dyson, *Darwin Among the Machines: The Evolution of Global Intelligence* (New York: Basic Books, 1998).

p. 148: Illustration an homage to Marv Wolfman and George Pérez's *New Teen Titans* character, Cyborg (1980). Also an homage to Leonardo da Vinci's *Vitruvian Man*, c. 1487.

p. 148: Ray Kurzweil, *The Singularity Is Near: When Humans Transcend Biology* (New York: Penguin, 2006).

p. 149, panel 1: Jaron Lanier, *You Are Not a Gadget: A Manifesto* (New York: Knopf, 2010).

p. 149, panel 3: Bill Joy, "Why the future doesn't need us: Our most powerful 21st-century technologies—robotics, genetic engineering, and nanotech—are threatening to make humans an endangered species," Wired.com, April 2000.

p. 149, panel 4: Abraham Maslow, "A Theory of Human Motivation," *Psychological Review* 50 (1943): 370–96.

I, MEDIA

pp. 150–51: Yochai Benkler, *The Wealth of Networks: How Social Production Transforms Markets and Freedom* (New Haven: Yale University Press, 2006).

p. 151, panel 1: Illustration after Henri Matisse, *Dance (II)* (1910).

pp. 152–53: Robert Wright, *Nonzero: The Logic of Human Destiny* (New York: Pantheon, 2000).

p. 154, panels 2–3: Neil Postman, *Amusing Ourselves to Death: Public Discourse in the Age of Show Business* (New York: Viking, 1985).

INDEX

JOSH NEUFELD is the author of the *New York Times* best-seller *A.D.: New Orleans After the Deluge*, which Wired.com called "a sterling example of comics with a social conscience." *Rolling Stone* called it "stunning." He is also the cocreator (with R. Walker) of *Titans of Finance: True Tales of Money and Business* and was a longtime artist for Harvey Pekar's *American Splendor*. He lives in Brooklyn, New York, with his wife, Sari Wilson.

www.joshcomix.com

BROOKE GLADSTONE is the cohost and managing editor of WNYC's *On the Media*, distributed by NPR. She has also served as NPR's media correspondent, Russia reporter, and senior editor of both *Weekend Edition* and *All Things Considered*. She has two Peabody Awards, a few Murrow Awards, the National Press Club's press criticism award, and was the recipient of a Knight Fellowship at Stanford University. She lives in Brooklyn, New York, with her husband, Fred Kaplan.